STREET SMARTS

101 Short Stories, Essays and Insights to Improve Communication Skills

Printed in the United States of America
First Printing, 2021

https://www.armanitalks.com

TABLE OF CONTENTS

AUTHOR'S PREFACE

Imagine a world without any boundaries.
0 *rules.*
0 *traditions.*
0 *cultural norms.*

Even a free-spirited individual may not like the sound of that. A world without any rules is begging for chaos. For any complex system (like a society) some rules are better than none. If you live in a well-off society, then it's easy to take small things for granted. Such as the roads...

Streetlights, clear boundaries on the road showing a separation in lanes, stop signs etc. These are all tools which help the driver navigate the streets. These serve as rules for all the other drivers who desire to travel from one spot to the next.

When the light is green, go.
When the light is red, stop.

Sure, every now and then, some drivers don't abide by these rules. But *'every now and then'* is better than *'always.'*

Now imagine a society that is not that well-off. They too have the streetlights, clear boundaries on the road showing a separation in lanes and stop signs. However, most of the drivers don't follow the rules.

They drive past the red light whenever they feel like it. There are tons of cars that drive in the middle of 2 lanes causing traffic jams. Plus, stopping at a stop sign is a laughable concept. You may think I'm joking, however, many countries around the world have roads that are the utmost chaos.

When you make eye contact with that chaos, you begin to appreciate boundaries that were once taken for granted.

The real world isn't always that pretty. It would be a Utopian world where there are boundaries for everything. Clear black and white ways of doing things.

Yet, that is not the case. This is the reason for injustices, someone getting the short end of the stick, betrayal and much more.

But a lack of boundaries does not always have to be terrifying. In plenty of occasions, a lack of rules can be used to your advantage. This book will get you thinking in a different way.

ARE BOUNDARIES AN ILLUSION?

After I graduated from college, I got a job in Sterling, Virginia. Most of my life had been spent in Florida. I had no clue where Sterling was, or if I even knew anyone there. I was starting over.

To make matters worse, my company said that I would be staying with a bunch of random people in a house until my training was complete. Really? Y'all can't even get me a solo apartment?

This was going to be tough.

The day I land in Virginia, a confused cab driver picks me up. He keeps asking me for directions and keeps hitting dead ends on the roads. After some time, he pulls up in front of the place that I am supposed to be staying at.

I thought this must have been some sort of a mistake.
It wasn't.

When I saw where I would be staying for the next couple of months, my sadness turned into joy.

I was going to be staying in a mansion. Sterling Virginia is one of the wealthiest spots in the United States.

It took some time for me to get comfortable with the roommates who had already built a friendship before me entering that day. Luckily, I was able to get closer with them as time passed on by.

The house had a dog named McDice. A beautiful German shepherd that was friendly and always down to play.

McDice was a part of the family in that household. He instilled a culture of us all having each other's backs, as strange as that sounds. Animals have the power to bond humans.

One day, something unusual happens.

McDice, who is normally super energetic, is low in energy. He seems almost lifeless. He is occupying a corner in the house and is not moving. The food remains untouched, and the water is still. What's going on?

The roommates were worried. We did some research on what could possibly be the issue, but we had no clue. It was time to take McDice to the vet.
Mariah, McDice's owner, went onto explain what was going on to the vet. The vet was a large man, roughly 6'5, broad shoulders with a British accent. He seemed like he hated his job.

He said he had no clue what was wrong with the dog and couldn't say what the next steps were until he ran some preliminary tests and did some x-rays. He wondered if McDice ate something that he wasn't supposed to.

When the vet gave the amount due to for the preliminary checkups, Mariah was crushed. It was a gargantuan amount that she simply could not afford. Not only that, even if the roommates were to pool their money together, we still couldn't afford it.

Did I mention we were not getting paid until we were done with the training? At this stage, we were all just running through our savings accounts.

Mariah begged the vet to lower the price, but he would not budge. He told us the vet offers a service to put dogs to sleep just in case we couldn't do anything.

This vet's lack of compassion was infuriating. However, he was just doing his job. Compassion was not in his rule book.

Time goes on by.

As we are talking about what the next step is, I decide to go to the parking lot to make sure my car didn't get towed. I had parked somewhere iffy.
While I'm walking to the car, this Russian girl comes to me. She was the quiet girl who was standing by the large vet.... observing.

She didn't say much, but you could tell she was listening.

She comes to me and asks, *'How much can you pay? I'm curious.'*
I was baffled that she asked me that question.

That's when she shaves off 500 dollars from the price the vet gave.
'Can you pay that?' she asked.

I loved her generosity, but we couldn't pay that. We had to go much lower. Maybe half of what the vet proposed. I shook my head in sadness.

'What about 1000 dollars off? Can you pay that?' the Russian girl asked.

She wanted to help. However, she wanted to help in a very private way. Otherwise, her boss could easily tell something fishy was going on. That's why I believe she approached me in a one-on-one setting.

After talking to her for some time, I eventually said, 'I'm sorry, but we are all broke at the moment. We don't have money during training. We just have enough to pay 50% of the bill.'

I thought the Russian girl would get furious for me proposing such a low number...but she didn't. She gave me the facial expression which indicated, *'Say no more.'*
Then left.

After 20 minutes, the Russian girl comes to the room with all the roommates and says, *'Hey, we looked and saw certain operations were not needed. This is the final bill.'*

This girl hands us a bill for 50% of what was initially proposed!!

The roommates could not believe it. It felt like a miracle had just been hand delivered to us. The Russian girl looked at me and made a sudden 'shh' motion with her index finger when the others were not looking, implying, *'don't say a word.'*

McDice was back to being healthy in a few days. It was nothing a few minor shots couldn't take care of.

That Russian girl showed me that boundaries are there, yes. But often, those boundaries are negotiable.

WHAT ARE STREET SMARTS?

When you envision street smarts, you may envision something dark. Images of someone robbing a bank, doing illegal activities, or manipulating others.

However, I do not view it like that. My definition of street smarts is:

The ability to adapt and thrive in a changing world.

This is the mindset of someone who is bold, has a quick bounce back rate from rejection, and regularly gathers practical life experiences.
Street smarts serve as practical problem solving that factor in emotions as well.

It's easy to be smart when there is not much pressure. When you are in a safe environment. However, the tables turn when you have to problem solve with your heart beating fast due to terror. That moment of terror will be presented many times in the real world.

A large part of street smarts comes down to communications skills.

The Russian girl who helped get the deal for the vet cost is not a rare character. Plenty of people will try to give you a helping hand when your back is against the wall. A mind that is not primed with the rulesets of 'street smarts' will be blind when those opportunities present themselves.

Other times, people who you thought you could rely on to the tee suddenly back stab you. Sometimes, it is right after you got done telling others about what a stand-up person this individual was.

Dualities exist.

Street smarts is about accepting the good and the bad.

It's about viewing the good and the bad in the same light, so this individual becomes unbreakable.

CAN STREET SMARTS AND BOOK SMARTS COEXIST?

Imagine you are waiting for a bus late at night. You are waiting in an extremely dangerous neighborhood with no one nearby.

Suddenly, a man dressed in all black starts walking towards you. He is holding a machete.
He asks, *'Would you like to keep your right arm or left arm?'*

In terror, you say, 'I want to keep both!'

Despite you being a right-handed individual, you still understand the value of your left hand. Both the arms complement one another. One side leads, the other side helps magnify.

That's the dynamic that street smarts and book smarts have with one another.

It's not a matter of putting them in competition. Instead, it's about finding unique ways to have them magnify one another.
Street smarts represent application.
Book smarts represent theory.
Combine both and create synergy.

With that being said, one side for the most part needs to lead. Which one is your right hand?

Traditionally, we are taught to lead with book smarts first. That's because it is easier to quantify book smarts. It is easier to see whether or not the kid passed the class and which letter grade they got.

It becomes much more difficult to measure the work ethic, discipline, and consistency they exhibited leading up to that grade.

Remember, street smarts are built through the lack of boundaries while book smarts are built by operating within boundaries. How is someone meant to combine these 2 disparate concepts?

Lead with 1 and fill in the gaps in understanding with the other.
Lead with street smarts and fill in the gaps in understanding with book smarts.

This creates a well-educated doer, rather than a savage who hasn't read a book in ages, or the 'know it all' with 0 skin in the game.

Having skin in the game requires street smarts leading the way. It's a game of doing, applying and taking purposeful action centered around a vison.

With targeted acts, it becomes much easier to find content that fits your life purpose, rather than just asking for random book suggestions for the sake of feeling smart.

Book smarts and street smarts can absolutely coexist. It's just about determining which one you want leading your life.

HOW THIS BOOK WORKS

This book is collection of my insights from the world of street smarts. You will learn practical concepts regarding public speaking, social skills, emotional intelligence, creativity, storytelling, and level up mindset.

These soft skills give you a deeper understanding of how to deal with the intricacies of human nature.

Each of the stories and essays are unrelated with one another. So, you can pick and choose whichever content you'd like to consume without the fear of missing something from a prior chapter.

The lessons in this book were learned the hard way. Some of the content has a step-by-step process of how I go about solving certain issues that pertain to street smarts.

Other parts of the book don't have a clear solution. This leaves the reader to assign their own meaning and get a stronger grasp of what they believe the moral was.

Most of the stories in this book are under 1000 words which makes it's a *short-short story* if we are being technical. I believe tiny tales are a weapon when it comes to learning because it fires a machine gun of ideas into the mind of the reader, which will make it stick.

BUILDING YOUR STREET SMARTS

A concept which is important in street smarts is 'resonation.' This is the art of meeting someone in a similar vibrational frequency.

I share the stories in this book from my firsthand perspective.

So rather than being given a lecture in the formal setting of PowerPoints, you can get a bird's eye view of someone else building their street smarts.

The journey of informal education never ends. It's only a journey that gets better with time.

To put into words what has no boundaries is a difficult task. It takes some time to get out of the school mindset of thinking 'x, y and z will give me x, y and z.' In the real world, 'x, y and z can give you 1, 5 and zebra.'

The world is unpredictable.
There is pain and there is joy.
There are ups and there are downs.
There is cowardice and there is bravery.

The nuances and the dynamics of these differences are what allows the human mind to extract meaning.

Building street smarts is learned the hard way. Where the masses mainly learn in a formal sense, the street smarts individual learns in a dynamic sense.

Being inflexible sounds great until you have your first encounter with the world being flexible. Unlike roads, life does not always have the streetlights, clear boundaries showing lanes and the stop signs. Plenty of lessons are up for interpretation.

So let these 101 short stories, essays and insights help you think in a different way.

Most of our lives, we led with book smarts. Now it's a new philosophy of leading with street smarts and sprinkling in books along the way.
This leads for a memorable journey and a holistic experience in the roads of life.

ARMANITALKS

THE PHOENIX

The Phoenix is a mythical bird that sets itself on fire only to rise back up again, stronger.

When I first heard the story of the Phoenix, I was amazed. An immensely powerful concept that represents a human.

What's even more fascinating is that there are multiple cultures around the world that have a similar Phoenix character in their stories. It's as though this bird is more than a bird.

In my first book, Level Up Mentality, I introduce the Phoenix & how us humans were destined to take up this role.

There is no choice. But we act like we a choice.
'What does that even mean?'
Well...

We have no clue how powerful we are until we have no choice but to be powerful.

I had a friend who was close to his brother. Like best friend status close.

A few years ago, his brother got sentenced to prison for over a decade due to a heinous crime. My friend was blindsided.

Out of nowhere, his brother was snatched away and now
their family was in shambles.

The next few years was a process of rebuilding for my
friend. The thing was, he had no other choice but to
rebuild.

His brother wasn't magically going to be released from
prison just because he was sad. So, my friend had to work
on himself & his life.

This was a case of the bird setting itself on fire.
Only to be reborn again.

The people who think they have a choice in the matter are
the ones who whine a lot.

*'Well, it's my brother's fault... It's the system's fault... I'm not
going to do anything about it...'*
So, they do nothing.

In the real world, doing nothing is doing something. Time
is being wasted regardless. Plus, all they are doing is
conditioning a victim mindset to their subconscious mind.

There are some individuals who let childhood traumas
radiate all the way to adulthood.
I feel for them.
It's sad.

There are other individuals who let their childhood traumas
propel them to new heights.
The road less taken.

It's less taken because being reborn after being burned feels like a rite reserved only for a mythical bird like the Phoenix. However, that's not accurate.

Humans become more powerful when they are stress tested and don't quit. Their skin toughens, mind sharpens & fire radiates.

We were all born to be the Phoenix at one point or another.

I don't trust people who have never been through a rock bottom moment. These people have had it too easy or are just unaware. Nothing real about them.

The world is intrigued by pain and how people overcame pain in a unique way.

Some become supreme athletes.
Others become supreme writers.
Others find a way to become something they never knew was possible.

Choose to be the Phoenix rather than devolving into someone who others pity. Nothing is sadder than the life of a victim.

Even if you feel like a victim of your circumstances, adopt the life of the Phoenix anyways.
Force yourself.

Reinforce epic images to the subconscious mind.
'For how long?'
Until you become epic yourself.

BEING A SURFER

I remember being a big Rocket Power fan growing up.
My brother was into Hey Arnold. Both shows were good.
The peak era of cartoons. But something about Rocket
Power was *different*.

The sports that the kids in the show were interested in
were way different than the sports that I was interested in.
I was interested in traditional sports like basketball &
football.

The kids in Rocket Power were interested in playing
hockey, skateboarding, and surfing. Something bout surfing
seems majestic.

Riding water.
Sort of like taming nature.
Or learning to work alongside it.

The kids in Rocket Power loved it when there were BIG
waves. They found it challenging. Since they were
confident in their skills, the big waves didn't bother them
one bit.

Communication skills = Surfing.

There was this yogi who was once asked how he was so
good at relaxing. He said that he surfs the game of life.

Despite dealing with negative thoughts, negative people &
negative experiences, he was able to ride the waves. The
bigger the waves, the better. Not bothered one bit.

The communications world has cool people.
Arrogant people.
A lot of snakes.

Just like the waters of an ocean are never still, humans are never predictable. If you are looking for ways to not encounter any negative individuals, then you'll be searching for a long time.

The correct question to ask yourself is:
'How well am I surfing this game we call life?'

Even if you never want to talk to someone again, you will find yourself talking to someone again.
'Are you saying I can never avoid humans?'
That is correct.

Communication is either happening actively or passively.
It can be something as active as breaking the ice with someone.
   • *Or something as passive as paying rent to a landlord.*
Humans aren't going to be going away anytime soon.

Just like thoughts are waves in the internal world.
Humans & experiences are waves in the external world.

Therefore, the only constant is YOU.
You, my friend, have no choice in this surfing matter.

When you have the mindset of a surfer, you start becoming bold like the kids in Rocket Power. The kids in Rocket Power weren't always riding the waves with grace.

There were times they would fall off their surfboard.

There will be times you lose your temper.
All good.

Get back on your board again.

You quit surfing once you die.
Till then, ride the tides & navigate with grace.

POWER OF A GREAT INTRODUCTION

For a business owner, getting a referral is a great feeling as long as the introduction was made correctly.
'What makes a great introduction?'
Let me tell you...

I was chilling after the gym.
Suddenly, I was sent over a referral.

This was a great referral.
My ideal target person to work with.
I set up a call to see what this fellow needed help with.

15 minutes into the call, the deal was closed, and the PayPal notification hit.
So seamless.

What made this close so easy?
Normally, it takes some time.
Not 15 minutes, but a few calls are required.

What made this close so easy was the pre-frame that led to the introduction.

My past client had gotten good results on his storytelling skills from our sessions. Therefore, when he referred me, he was able to speak about those results.

After hearing about my past client's results, the referral was pretty much sold. There was no selling needed from my end.
Just a little bit of educating on the process.

The pre-frame is an important social concept.
It is how you introduce before introducing.

Let's say you're a college guy who is trying to hook up with some girls and you're going from party to party.

If a group of girls are talking about you and are like, 'Hey, Johnny is so cute. All the girls seem to love him on campus.'

Now you have a much higher chance of getting a date. Why? It's because these girls talked you up. They pre-framed you in a positive light. This is even before a formal introduction has been made.

That's why I call a pre-frame the introduction BEFORE an introduction.

Let's flip this scenario.
If all the girls were like, 'Johnny is the creepiest guy on this campus. I get weird vibes from him.'
Now it's a completely different story.

The pre-frame is negative. Therefore, you may have more resistance in getting a date with this select group of girls.

To illustrate this point further, pre-framing is highly relevant in the world of public speaking.

This is why it's wise for a speaker to have a strong
introduction ready to give to the host.
The speaker should be their own hype man.

Once the host reads off the introduction, the speaker pulled
off a chess move. The audience has been warmed up, which
will make them much more receptive to the speech.

The power of pre-framing is amazing when we have a
personal experience with it. Plus, it shows social
intelligence when we do it for others.
When creating a pre-frame for others, we automatically
increase our social value!

What is social value?
It is a form of perception.

The person who referred me that client raised his social
value in my eyes. Due to the law of reciprocation, I wanted
to return a favor for him. This is why a big part of charisma
just comes down to spreading good energy.

The pre-frame is a cheat code to hacking likability.
Referring people business is an evergreen skill that will last
another 10 lifetimes.

I know this guy who is super awkward. But he is a referral
machine. Always giving people business because of the
industry that he works in.

You think the people who are getting referrals from him
care that he is socially awkward?
Nope.
There are many ways to be charismatic.

Plenty of opportunities to go around.

-You can be funny.
-Know how to be a great listener.
-A stellar pre-framer etc.

An attractive personality is learning the art of giving before getting. How one gives is completely up to them, their comfort levels & their areas of interests.

ENGINEERING &

PSYCHOLOGY

It's hard for the mind to grasp something when it doesn't have pictures. The pictures, metaphors & similes are what allows the mind to make an ambiguous concept, concrete.

A while back, I was reading Keith Ferrazzi's book, Never Eat Alone. It is a book with practical tips on how to network with others.

Keith is regarded as a 'professional networker.' I never knew such a position existed. But while reading the book, I knew the man knew what he was talking about.

He made me think of networking in a new light.

As I was reading the book, I could not help but notice the similarities of a social network & an internet network. How we are all 1 person away from knowing 1,000 others & 2 people away from knowing a million others.

Same concept in how a message is spread in a node.

This demonstrates why word of mouth is so popular.
It gets a flurry of business coming our way and the online internet business starts seeing a snowball of success.

This made me realize that technology is simply the nature that humans have created. We made it as a mirror of us.

If you want to learn a lot about yourself, study the computer hardware, software & network theory.

'Example?'
Sure.

When I was using my laptop late last year, I realized how slow it was. I was getting an internet connection. But it was so slow that it felt good as useless.

Not going to lie, but that moment made me start taking my health more seriously.
'What???'
Yes, no lie.

- o   The physical laptop is like your body. It holds the **CPU** which is your brain.
- o   The internet serves as the mind.
- o   And the user (yourself) is consciousness.

My consciousness could have been sharp, and the mind could have been working well... But if the laptop is slow, then it is annoying & makes my production suffer.

It negatively affects the mind followed by the consciousness. Starts a toxic loop.

Imagine how many people are well read, talented and skilled. But they are fat as shit.

Just imagine how slow their computer is running.

They are working with dial up when they could be working with high-speed internet.

Another example is giving **2** people the same exact laptop.
But one uses it to watch porn. While the other uses it to
build a business.
Why?

It's because the users are different.
The consciousness levels between the **2** individuals are on a
different spectrum.

One is not self-aware at all.
The other is highly self-aware.

This holds true in the psychology world as well.

2 people who come from the ghetto, were broke, poor
household etc. But their lives are different. One felt
defeated, became a drug dealer, and went to prison. One
felt empowered to start a new story, worked hard, became
a CEO in his firm and gave back to the community.

Same circumstances, different perceptions.

If you are a logical person looking to learn more about
psychology, look at the tangible world. Look at the
relationship between technology and humans.

When learning something for the first time, it helps having
your perception engaged.

Since psychology is the study of the mind, it is not always
easy to see. All good. Start with the tangible & work your
way to the intangible.

CURIOSITY = LIFETIME GROWTH MODE

We spend so many years being programmed that it's crazy. This is one of the main reasons that I don't know if I'm going to send my future kids to school.

Homeschooling has always sounded rather good to me. *Why?*

It's because the school system misguides us on what intelligence means. For years & years I was programmed into thinking that I was stupid.
'How come?'
Because I was an awful test taker.

I would study for hours & hours in preparation for an exam. Thought I hit all the major points & felt confident.

However, on the day of an exam? My confidence wasn't quite there & I ended up getting a subpar score.

This annoyed me.
Was this it?
Is this how life was going to be?
I guess I'm never going to be 'smart.'

OFF TO THE REAL WORLD

Once I graduated from college, I entered the real world.

Entering the real world allowed me to completely shift my mindset. The main reason for that was because of freedom.

You see, I realized in the real world that I wasn't dumb, I just wasn't curious during my time in school.

How could I be?
Getting a bunch of subjects that I had o desire to learn being shoved into my world was not appealing.

Which is why learning felt like work.
But in the real world?
Exact opposite.
Now I had the freedom to follow my curiosities & design my own life curriculum.

WHY CURIOSITY IS KING

-Gut instinct is your body trying to tell you something.
-Curiosity is your mind trying to tell you something.

In today's era, it's easier than ever to follow your curiosities.

Information is abundant. Which is why curiosity serves as a life compass. Want to know what's sad? There are tons of people who don't follow their curiosities. They think they have learned it all.
Ha!!

It's laughable for someone to think that but stupidity will amaze you.

Thinking you 'know it all' is a very destructive belief to have.

Lack of curiosity leads to a fixed mindset.

Abundance of curiosity leads to a growth mindset.

THE REAL SIGN OF INTELLIGENCE

In my humble opinion, test scores are not what measures intelligence.
Curiosity does.

I'm a firm believer that people can learn anything that they have the desire to. Once you get out of school, education does not stop. It is just beginning.

- Self-education = Fulfillment 101.

Are you someone who has been maximizing your resources to optimize your curiosity? Or have you settled into the abyss?

Leverage your curiosity correctly or you will self-destruct.
'Self-destruct??'
Yes. Want to know a secret?
'Sure.'
Humans are naturally curious creatures. It's primal. Which is why a little kid is always asking questions nonstop. It is ingrained in us.

But when you are not curious about stuff that can help you level up, you start getting curious about nonsense.
Gossip, political scandals, drama etc.

Which is why it's smart to:

1. Show humility & understand that you don't know a
fraction of what there is to know.

2. Put energy into curiosities that help you level up.

3. Learn away.

This easy 3 step formula will have you growing like none
other.

Give it a try & you'll realize how much you can stretch
your mind to new heights.

WHAT THE BACKSTREET BOYS TAUGHT ME ABOUT LIFE

When I first moved into the US, the Backstreet Boys were huge. Everyone was listening to them in my class. The boys and the girls. Even the teachers were listening to them.

As the years went by, people began evolving. Backstreet Boys were no longer cool.

If you were a boy who listened to them, you were called 'gay' by the other boys in the class. Being a foreign kid who wasn't aware of much cultural lingo, I had no clue how a music preference meant I was gay.

The other 7-year-olds would find kids who listened to the Backstreet Boys & openly mocked them.

Linkin Park & Eminem were now considered cool.

Who decided what was cool or not?
Being a youngster, I was like, *'okay I'll play along with this.'*
So, I stopped listening to the Backstreet Boys.

By the time I got into high school & began playing basketball, a part of me needed a hype song to get amped up. My heart told me to listen to 'Larger than Life.'

But then my rational mind was like, *'Whoa there bucko!
Don't forget it's not cool.'*
So, I found another track to listen to.

As a few weeks passed, I decided enough was enough.

I was going to download a few Backstreet Boys songs on
my iPod & change the names so no one could tell.

One day, I was in the locker room with the other guys
getting ready for gym class. You could tell I was getting
hyped. This caught the attention of a kid named Chris.

Chris came up to me and was like, 'Armani, what are you
getting so hyped about? Let me listen!'

Just like that, he grabs one ear bud and begins listening
along. He listened for a few before he was able to make out
what song it was. I tried to skip forward to the next track.

But it was too late.

Chris's fatass was already blurting out, 'Hey guys!! Armani
is listening to the Backstreet Boys. Hahaha.'

The entire locker room busted out in laughter.
They all clowned me & said I had the music taste of a girl.
I was very embarrassed.

Until I wasn't.

At that point, I realized I had spent years avoiding this
band whose music I enjoyed. All for what? So a bunch of
other kids wouldn't judge me?

What a foolish mistake.

That locker room moment allowed me to feel as though an anchor had been removed internally. A lot of kids from my locker room came later to me in silence and said:
'I love the Backstreet Boys too. Just didn't want anyone to know. What's your favorite song?'

I realized that caring about other people's opinions like that is always a losing game.

They ain't living in my shoes. Nor am I living in theirs.

They can have all the opinions they want. But at the end of the day, if it ain't helping me, then I ain't letting it influence me.

What is your Backstreet Boys moment?
What is it that you are hiding for fear of embarrassment?

Now let me ask you.
Will these people matter in 5 years?
Do these people even matter now?

Remember this OG, you don't just stop caring about opinions out of the blue moon. It is a very painful process.

Those who survive will tell you it's 100% worth it.

PLANTING THE SEEDS FOR YOUR FUTURE

There was once a funny post that popped up on my Instagram. It dealt with old school basketball vs new school basketball.

The post was comparing basketball from the 1960s to basketball in the 2000s. This post was making a mockery out of 1960s basketball.

Showing a bunch of unathletic players in short shorts, missing easy layups & looking foolish. The next video right after it was a clip of the most athletic superstars in the 2000s era.

The post was trying to imply that the competition nowadays is much more elevated than the 60s. Was the post wrong?
Probably not.

The game of basketball has elevated tremendously in terms of technology, sports nutrition, and workouts within the past few decades.

It's not outlandish to say that the rise in sports medicine & technology could breed new superstars that were unprecedented in the 60s.

But guess what?
'What?'
The post was still misguided.

'How? You just said basketball nowadays may be more athletic than the 60s.'
I did.
But why are we comparing the 2 in the same context?

That's like me saying:
'I bet you walked way better now than you did when you were a toddler.'

Sure, that is true.
But why is that comparison being made?

The reality is...
The players in the 60s were planting the seeds for the future.

They were laying down the groundwork so the game of basketball could be built on a strong infrastructure.

It's also like saying:
'I bet Lebron had more Instagram followers than Michael Jordan.'
Sure, but what's your point?

It's fun to make simplified debates in sports.
It's able to spark discussion for hardcore & general fans.

However, in terms of life, planting the seeds & watering it is a slow process.

In my backyard at West Palm Beach, I planted a tiny plant when I was in the 7th grade. Nowadays, when I go home, the tiny plant is a huge tree.

Seeing the transformation happen in real time got me to see
how nature relates to people.

A digital version of that change is in Amazon.
When Amazon first launched its website, it was so ugly.

Nowadays, the website has evolved. It's one of the most
user-friendly digital interfaces out there.

Calling it ugly is shortsighted.
Because it was just the seed in the initial stages.
Now it has matured into something greater.

The odd thing about seeds is that we have no option but to
plant them.

Seeds for our life are skills & habits that we repeat a bunch
of times. It may just be a seed now. But over time, it will
turn into something much grander. (Yes, this applies for bad
habits as well).

When planting the seeds for the future, it's smart to
practice decade-by-decade thinking.
What are you investing in?
Will it be relevant in another 10 years?

Sort of like the NBA.
I doubt the league managers were like:
'Let's start this league so we can pay our rents till lease is
up!'

If that was their mentality, we would never have had Wilt,
Kareem, Magic, MJ & Kobe.

When envisioning the long term, losses morph from
roadblocks to mere speedbumps.
Call that a mindset shift.

Consciously plant the seeds.
Water them with enthusiasm.
As time elapses, the tree will arise from the ground.

SILENT MAJORITY

In the world of content creation, there is a group known as the silent majority.

'The silent majority?'

That's correct.

The silent majority of the content creation world is the group of people who watch, hear & read all of your stuff. Yet, they never interact with your stuff.

So, you have no clue they are there.

But they are there.

I discovered the silent majority when I started getting clients from my ArmaniTalks brand.

Every now and then, I'd post a tweet saying that I am taking on new clients and to book a free consult call to see if we are a good fit.

One person who booked a call was a 65-year-old lawyer who said he bookmarks each of my tweets.

I asked him what his Twitter handle was?

He gave it to me.

It was an anonymous account that was following 200 people & had 2 followers. No tweets, mainly retweets.

At first glance, the account looked like a bot.

Talking to the account holder gave me clarity. It showed me that behind these accounts are people who heard me and watched me.
We worked together for a best man speech that he had coming up.

I wondered how many more accounts like that were out there. Then I thought about it... I do the same thing!

As I have been growing my YouTube channel, I have been watching more videos on YouTube tips. One girl I am subscribed to is a girl named Annie. Each of her videos are highly informative.

After watching her videos, I always learn something new. However, after watching her videos, I don't engage.

That's not how I use YouTube.
I just use it to watch or make videos myself.

Annie probably has no clue that I exist.
I am simply a silent majority to her.

Everyone uses social media differently.
Some use it to lurk.
Others use it to learn.
Others use it to lurk, learn, engage etc.

Social media is a powerful tool. A tool that can spread messages to multiple parties of all shapes and sizes.

One thing with the digital world is that it is quick to take away the humanization.
'Meaning?'

Meaning that it's easy to see numbers instead of people.

Let's say you are an upcoming Twitter account with 1,500
followers. You may think:
'Well, there are so many bigger accounts.'

But 1,500 is nothing to scoff at! That's like 3 wedding
sized audiences. And these people are curious about what
you have to say.

The silent majority is spilling over.

Although you may not hear them...
Although you may not see them....
Although you may have no clue they exist....

They are paying attention.
Be consistent & produce with abundance.

THE MIDGET

In the 10th grade, I was the shortest kid in my class. Not only was I short, but I was skinny. Not only was I short & skinny, but my fashion was off too.

I had one thing that I had going for me.
'What was that?'
Basketball.
'What made you get into basketball?'
Good question....

During the years of high school, a lot of my close friends were towering over me. I remember I was also the shortest in my house as well.

One day, my dad & grandpa gave me advice. It was identical advice. They told me if I wanted to get taller, then I needed to play basketball.

'Look how tall the players in the NBA are. You know how they got like that? It's because they played basketball' they said.
Oh yea?

I shot around, but it was nothing too serious. Are you telling me I can get taller if I play basketball??
I was sold.

For the next few months, I invested in basketball. Would play every single day after school. On the weekends, I would play for hours.

Many of my friends asked me why I was playing so much.

I told them it was my only shot to getting tall. They looked at me like I was crazy. But I looked at them like they had no clue.

Week after week, I played.

Took it so seriously that I bought ankle weights to make it tougher on me. My game improved. Slowly, something else had improved too...

My house had a fridge that I was always shorter than. Once I began playing a lot of basketball, I noticed I was starting to close the gap. I don't know if the fridge was getting shorter or if I was getting taller!

As the summer started to wrap up, I was reborn. I was no longer this 5'3 guy. Now I was 6'0.

By the time I had returned to school, my friends couldn't believe it. I had overtaken all of them out of nowhere! The crazy look that they had earlier turned into intrigue.

What happened?

Looking back, it's evident that basketball wasn't the reason I got taller. It was just puberty, right? Otherwise, anyone playing basketball would be tall.
I don't know fam...

A part of me still thinks there was something meta-physical involved. In my mind, I had this belief that I was going to get taller.

I had no clue my dad & grandpa were telling me something
to motivate me. I thought it was a fact. There was no
doubt in my mind that it was going to happen.

*When I had that belief mixed with harmonious actions, it was
as though I had set off a different force.*

The moral of the story is not about the height. It's about
intense belief. View your wildest dreams as a fact. The
belief is what allows you to push on even when people look
at you all crazy.

I believe that my intense thought patterns vibrated into my
body & led to the transition in height.

But who knows? Maybe I'm talking crazy right now.

Truth is, you need some crazy in you.

I couldn't speak in front of 1 person without fidgeting and
getting nervous when I was a youngster. But I knew one
day I would be speaking in front of 500 people with ease.

Crazy? Absolutely.
But did it happen? Absolutely.

Look around you.
Heck, look at the device you are reading this from.

Pretty sure our ancestors would view us as crazy for
thinking we can have digital devices that could transmit
energy. Until we did it. The human race has been

responsible for marvelous innovations. All it takes is for thoughts & behaviors to align.

That's when we unlock the potential to join the Mount Rushmore of human history.

UNLOCK YOUR

CREATIVITY

When was the last time you utilized your imagination?
'Does daydreaming count?'
No.
'Then not much Armani.'
Tsk tsk... Big mistake.
'Why? Creativity is for little kids anyways. What good will it serve me in the real world?'
It will serve you a lot.

It's sad, but we have completely misunderstood the power of creativity. And can you blame us?

We go from creative mega houses as children to being put in school. Once we are in school, we suppress the creativity & overpower our brains with logic. We are given tons & tons of information that we are told to learn, just so we can use it to pass an exam.

We go years & years like this.

We come out of our schooling environments to now enter the workforce. Another factory of logic where we are doing tasks. But this is a big mistake!

'Why? I can't see how creativity has anything to do with my everyday life.'
You don't.... yet. But you will... Trust me... you will...

WHAT IS CREATIVITY?

Creativity is the ability to produce imaginative & innovative ideas. Every human is creative.

'Even me???'

Yes, even you.

If you do not think you are creative, I want you to take a walk down memory lane. Remember when you were a child?

'Yep.'

You remember how you would spend hours imagining cool stuff, playing with action figures as if they were real people & make up a bunch of games with your friends?

'Yep.'

Well, that is all creativity.

However, the only thing is that you were utilizing your creativity to have fun, not change the world.

'Creativity to change the world? Is that even possible?'

It most certainly is.

CREATIVITY TO LEAVE A LEGACY

The light bulb, airplane & computer. What do all of these have in common?

'Uh....'

They were innovative creations just like anything on this planet. Let's zone in on the airplane.

You think the Wright Brothers were met with welcoming arms when they said they were going to create a device that will fly in the sky?

'No man. They were probably called crazy.'
So why did they pursue it?
'Beats me.'

They pursued it because their creativity allowed them to make eye contact with the impossible. Even though other people thought they were crazy, they saw their vision. That was an innovative idea that their creative brain produced.

Once the idea was grasped, their logical brain devised a plan to make it happen. And *now?* The Wright brothers are immortal, while their naysayers are forgotten.

Who got the last laugh?
'The creative ones.'
Correct. That is how you utilize your creativity to change the world.

WHAT HAPPENS IF YOU DON'T USE YOUR CREATIVITY?

'I never thought of it like that!! But I need to ask... What happens if I don't utilize my creativity?'
Something dangerous happens.
'Dangerous?'
Yes. Your creativity becomes monstrous.

The fact that we were imagining stuff since we were little kids shows something:
Logic is taught, but creativity is our natural way of existence.

We were born to utilize our imagination. But when you do not utilize it productively, something dark happens.

Your creativity meets the negativity bias.
If you do not know what the negativity bias is, it's when your brain naturally focuses on the negatives of your life for survival purposes.
It is a primal way of thinking that allowed our ancestors to survive.

However, the negativity bias is not as needed in today's society since we are not dealing with being eaten by a sabretooth tiger out of nowhere.

'Blah blah blah. Why are you bringing all this up for Armani?'
Because when creativity meets the negativity bias, you get anxiety.

When you do not use your imagination for good, it defaults to negative thinking patterns. Results?

- Creative ways for you to be negative.
- Creative ways for you to plan out your failures in advance.
- Creative ways for you to self-destruct your life.

Life doesn't have to be this way for you.

You can still change today & etch your name in history with the Wright brothers. You can still use your creativity to make an impact on this world.

UNLOCK YOUR CREATIVITY

So, we are going use our imagination for good. The exercises that I am going to give you will sound very unorthodox, but that's the point.

Remember earlier how I was saying that logical people were thinking that the Wright brothers were crazy? Well, a little crazy is needed for creativity.

It allows you to create unique, innovative ideas.

So here it goes:

1. Read Fiction: Reading fiction (science fiction preferred) forces your brain to work. Your brain is turning regular words into images that are out of this planet.

Your imagination will be forced to step up & do a lot of the heavy lifting. Think of this as a workout for your brain.

2. Creative Writing: For this one, you need to exercise your right brain some more. I want you to think about the most random topics that you can think about & force yourself to write 1-2 pages on it.

Ex: An elephant wanted to begin a journey to turn into a dragon. Explain why & how in a story format.

This exercise is tough in the initial stages. But it forces you to channel your imagination towards a final product. Push through.

3. Artistic Outlet: This one is optional but recommended. An artistic outlet can be learning an instrument, painting, creating new recipes.

This helps you go from consumer -> producer mode. While doing this, you take a lot of energy from your internal world & place it to the external world.

Remember, too much energy in the internal world overloads you & causes anxiety. So, release the energy.

CHANGED LIFE?

That is how you use your creativity to change the world.

'Gotcha bro! Is there any particular lane I should go on? Should I become an inventor like the Wright brothers or a storyteller like you?'
No set lane homie!

You can choose whatever works for you. Heck, you can even stick to your current job or business & use your creative powers to level up those facets of your life.

A few years ago, a journalist asked 50+ CEOs what they believe is the top trait of future CEOs. Guess what the majority said?
'Uh....'
Fool! Have you not been paying attention? They all said creativity.

It doesn't matter what lane you are in; creativity will always be a superpower that helps you level up.

STINGY WITH INFORMATION

Intent is a big thing in the social world. It shows the difference between a snake and a person who committed an honest mistake.

Sometimes the intent was harmless.
Sometimes the intent was harmful.

I used to know this guy named Thomas who knew how to solve the Rubik's cube.

Him effortlessly solving the cube got my curiosity. How did he do that? I was curious because I saw Will Smith solving it in the Pursuit of Happiness.

When I asked Thomas, he wouldn't tell me. He gave a vague response like:
'You know, I just learned.'

Alright buddy.
Not much help, but all good.

Actually, not all good.

This was bothersome to me. I wanted to learn how to solve this cube. But I didn't want to pester Thomas.

Not sure why I would have to pester him. Like a dummy, I realized that I could just Google it. Take a little initiative, you know. And that's what I did.

From Google, I was led to YouTube. That's when I
found a video of a guy solving the cube. He solved it in 6
minutes step by step. I watched that video many times.

In a few weeks, I was able to solve it as well.
Fascinating.

When others would ask me how I learned, I
enthusiastically referred the 6-minute video I watched.
'You guys should check out this link. All the steps are
there!'

I knew these people who were asking me wouldn't check
out the video though. Much love for them. But doubt they
had the desire to learn to solve it.

It was just a casual question.

This casual question got my attention. When they initially
did ask me that question, there was a micro move in me
that was like:
'Man, I Googled it & had to find the right video for me.
Why don't you take some initiative? Bum.'

That micro move was immediately overwhelmed by the
flurry of desire to recommend the video.
Yet, the micro move was noticed.

I think a part of Thomas found it disrespectful I asked him
how to solve the Rubik's cube. In his world, he probably
felt that I was undermining his success. He wanted to give
this illusion of knowing how to solve a cube. Solving the
cube is often seen as a symbol of being smart.

Now here comes a guy asking him to mechanically give the
answer which will take away the mystery.

I did the Rubik's cube in front of many people since then.
Normally through the following challenge:
'Yea right, you can't solve that!'

When it's solved, the general public is impressed.
While every now and then, a stickler is like:
'Yea, I'd know how to do it too if I followed it step by
step on YouTube.'

Marginalizing the win.

I believe this is what Thomas was afraid of. So I can't hate
on him.

I don't believe his intent was malicious.
I don't think he was even trying to teach me a lesson.

*'You know, I need to teach this Armani guy the art of doing his
own research.'*
Doubt he ever thought that.

Thomas does not embody any kind of intent. He did teach
me about a philosophy:
The art of sharing.

As resources become rich in this world, a lot of things will
become automated.

Information is rising.
It's a form of wealth.

Not any kind of information.
Information relevant to someone's life.

2 groups are emerging:
-The learned individuals who enjoy sharing.
-The learned individuals who do not enjoy sharing.

I share for a selfish and selfless reason.

Selfish, because it conditions my mind to have an abundance
mindset regarding ideas. Selfless, because it helps others.

Thomas's do exist in the ecosystem. I believe they serve
their role in the unique information landscape. I call them
the resistors. The components which are meant to slow
things down.

Sometimes, giving people clear information is a waste of
time.
'Why?'
Because clear information cannot be perceived by a
muddied mind.

Maybe Thomas *was* trying to teach me a lesson. Maybe he
was seeing if I would have the drive to do
my own research.
Maybe, just maybe, he wanted the next person who joined
the Rubik's cube fraternity...To earn it.

Rather than it being delivered on a silver spoon.

UNLEARN

'I think you got the title wrong.'
Nope, got it right.
'You wrote *unlearn.*'
Exactly.

Unlearning is a lot harder than learning.
When you get out there in the real world, you are going to
have to unlearn...a lot.

The first time I realized this was when I was working a
corporate job. Thought it was strategic to be very formal.
So that's how I carried myself.

As the new employee, I remember getting introduced to a
lot of the other people in the company. Something about a
few of them seemed so nonchalant. So informal.

Those fools. Didn't they realize the error in their ways?
Why weren't they carrying themselves in a more proper
manner??

For the next few weeks, I carried myself the way that we
were taught in school.

Be professional, they said.
And professional, I was.

But something didn't feel right.
'What was wrong?'
I felt secluded.

I noticed that the informal guys were buddying up to the higher ups.

-Making inside jokes.
-Going to team lunches.
-Telling stories.

While I & a lot of the other professional workers didn't see much (if any) social success.

Were we great at our jobs? Sure. However, we were often not recognized for it. That's when I began realizing something.
'Which was?'
People were never meant to be *professional*.

Let me clarify. I am not telling you to be unprofessional. Or some slob with little decorum. All I'm saying is to loosen up.

Loosening up was something that we were never taught in school. It was actually discouraged.

'Raise your hand before you speak' is the clearest example. It gives you the illusion that the real world is linear. That every speaking opportunity happens one at a time.

In school, that works.
In the real world, you'll be seen as too passive.

Loosening up comes down to talking to a person's child side.

Speak to someone's adult side to build an acquaintance.

Speak to someone's child side to build a friend.

A child is the purest form of loosening up.

They haven't been conditioned with too many rules.
They have no clue what professional even means.

There's a time to be professional & formal. *Take care of business.*
There's a time to melt the professionalism away. *Build some relationships.*

Friendships are not built by focusing on saying the 'right' things.
* 1 laugh generated > 100 well-structured sentences. Not even close.

In order to unlearn, you just need to analyze your experiences. We are all different. Which part of your life do you think is faulty? Then see how others may be carrying themselves for a little bit of inspiration.

In my case, I noticed I couldn't make friends in the workplace, and I saw the people who could. Noticed they were more relaxed & didn't take themselves so seriously. Then I got inspiration.

After that, it's a trial-and-error thing. You don't just magically unlearn overnight. It's something that happens overtime. A gradual implementation of renewed behaviors.

All about the reps.
Consistently.

Then out of nowhere, one day, you have AWARENESS
to the fact that your behavior has shifted. You will think it
happened suddenly. But no...
Look closer.

You were working routinely & your effort paid off.

It's sort of like trying to open the lid off a soda bottle. But
it's super tight.
Joe tries. Fails.
Bill tries. Fails.
Rick tries. Fails.
But when Steve tries? Success.

Steve didn't do it by himself. A combination of Joe, Bill,
Rick and Steve led to the success.

Same with all the days in a week. One day in the week will
not do it. Instead, a combination of the hours, days, weeks,
months, years....

Will finally lead to your Eureka Moment.
Amazing.

TRUST THE PROCESS >

RUSH THE PROCESS

I used to hate LeBron James. Nothing personal against the guy. He was just compared too much to my favorite player, Kobe Bryant.

LeBron fans would always call Kobe a ball hog & I had to get in endless debates with them. That soured my perception of LeBron at an early age.

But for the past few years, LeBron has been a source of inspiration.
'What changed?'
It's because he trusted the process.

If you are not a basketball fan, let me just give you a brief history of his career.

LeBron was drafted by his hometown team, Cleveland Cavaliers, in 2003.

Before he played a single game in the NBA, he had already signed a multi-million-dollar shoe deal, got endorsements & was dubbed as the next big thing etc. Let's just say that came with a lot of pressure.

'Would he live up to expectations?'
Yessir. He was lighting up the NBA in his second year.

Was able to pass, rebound, assist, play defense and so much more.

For years & years, he made the Cavaliers relevant.

'That's awesome!'
But there was a problem.
'And what was that?'
He was unable to get a championship.

With all this hype, it was seen as a foregone conclusion that
he would stack up championships. Well, where were they?
7+ years in the league and not 1 ring?? A lot of pressure
was being set up for LeBron.

At the time, the Cavaliers team was abysmal & winning
with them seemed murky. It was hard to blame LeBron.
But now the question was, where would he sign for the
free agency coming up?

In the summer of 2010, LeBron set the entire NBA world on fire.

He shocked the world by letting them know that he was
going to be leaving the Cleveland Cavaliers for the Miami
Heat. The Heat already had Dwyane Wade and Chris
Bosh.

This would mean adding LeBron to the Heat would form
a 3 headed monster. The entire NBA competitive landscape
had been put in jeopardy. Results?
LeBron tarnished his reputation.

He went from being the chosen one to the hated one.
Arena after arena would boo him.
They would throw vicious insults at him.

To make matters worse, his hometown of Cleveland had turned on him, calling him every name in the book & burning his jersey.

'Wow, that's bad!!'

No. What's worse was that everyone expected him to win multiple championship rings with the Heat. But he came up short.

In the 2011 Finals, he lost to the underdog Dallas Mavericks & put up an abysmal performance in the 6-game series.

LeBron's tarnished reputation just became 10x worse.

He was now seen as a choke artist. One of the worst labels you can throw at an athlete.

'If LeBron is such a failure, why are you inspired by him?' Because he wasn't a failure. He was simply going through the process.

After that horrendous playoff moment, LeBron went on to make 8 straight NBA finals and win 3 NBA championship rings. He has scored 30,000+ points, accumulated 8,000+ assists & snagged 8,000+ rebounds.

However, his accolades do not stop on the court.

He is a man of the community, participates in charities & started a school in his hometown for underprivileged kids. His career thus far has been nothing short of stunning.

What can you learn from this?

Well, imagine if LeBron quit after his Mavericks failure.
Imagine if he began to half ass during practice & pout?
Then, he would have never won anything.

The world does not favor people who half ass something.
Either go all in on or don't even bother.

This isn't to say just focus on your craft & ignore all other
parts of your life. But it is to say when you practice &
work, practice & work.

Have an end goal in mind and remain present while
working. That's how you trust the process.

LeBron had to spend 7+ years in the league before he won
his first championship. 7 plus years! Most people can't even
last 7 months.

That's perspective.

LeBron inspires me because the good and bad from his
career has been displayed on center stage. Imagine if there
was a film crew recording your good and bad days at work.

Observing each one of your moves.
Breaking down each failure to the tee.
Pretty daunting, right?

Well, that has been Lebron's world for the better part of
his life.

There are inspirational people in this world.

Don't just learn from their wins.
But observe carefully how they persevere despite a loss.

The first will speak to your mind.
The second will speak to your heart.

-If you are currently working on something, then double down.
-If you are not currently working on something, then find something to work on.

Idle hands create bums.

LeBron is still going, let's see how his career plays out. But even when he hangs up the jersey, he will continue to inspire millions from around the planet with the attitude he cultivated during his hardships.

Are Humans Naturally Good or Bad?

Some believe that we are born with human nature and that makes us animal like creatures. Others believe we are born divine creatures and have the propensity to be corrupted due to a lack of knowledge.

'What do you think?'
I don't know.

However, I have noticed a few things.

There was a day when I went to 7/11 to get some gas. I parked my car in front of a pump & began walking in.

15 feet in front of me, there was this old lady walking with a cane. As she was about to get on the step to walk into the store...
She falls.

The cane slips out of her hand, and she falls on her back. Making a loud thud.

There was no one near her at the time. My first response was to go help her up. As I am getting closer to her, I see 3 other people come rushing out of the 7/11 to help her up as well.

It was a Black guy in his 30s and a Spanish lady in her 40s
with her daughter.

At that point, I catch up & we try helping this lady out.

We do a small game plan.

-The Spanish lady is going to call the ambulance.
-The little girl is going to grab a bottle of water from the store.
-And me and the guy are going to take this lady to her car where
we are going to wait with her.

20 minutes passes on by & the ambulance comes. They do
some checkups & take the older lady to the hospital.

Then me & the others are about to head out. Before we
head out, we acknowledge what just happened.

In a sudden moment, a Bengali, Spanish lady + her
daughter & a Black man, united.

From the outside looking in, we looked different.
But deep inside?
We were the same.

None of us thought twice about helping the old woman
out.
It was muscle memory. Like we were born with the ability
to help. Not sure what to make of it.

I don't want to say that we are naturally good because
there were some people in the gas station who saw what
happened and went on minding their own business.

I don't want to call them bad people. They may have had places to go.

Deep inside, if you were to ask me for my theory...
I'm going to say that we are naturally good creatures.

Every time I hit a tough moment in my life where I had no choice but to wait it out, I became more compassionate.

Sort of like when all the derivatives are stripped away, the real human side shows its face.

DOING THINGS
DIFFERENTLY

In my neighborhood in Tampa, there are a lot of stray cats around the area. Most of the stray cats have nothing unique about them. They just look like regular cats.

But there is one particular cat that is different. It is a fat orange cat. Sort of looks like Garfield.

A few of the residents in my neighborhood play with this cat. They feed it. And the cat plays back with them. Very chill.

One day, I was going for a walk, and I see the fat orange cat looking at me.

As I was walking on my path, the cat didn't move. It just stood there & kept holding eye contact with me. This cat had guts.

Most of the other stray cats would just run away when a person was anywhere near them. But this cat stood its ground.

I looked at it.
And it kept looking back at me like it had me all figured out.

I then began to wonder...
How the hell did this cat get fat in the first place?

It's a stray.
It doesn't have an owner.
How is it gaining weight??

That's when I began to realize something.

This cat was different.
It was different by being itself.

Typically, most of our fears come from judgment. When you break down judgment, it comes down to being different. Being different in one way or another.

A lot of friendships break apart due to the fear of being judged & judging others. I know people who break apart years of a friendship because one person secretly supports a political candidate that the other person despises. A lot of people spend years hiding these secrets.

The fear of being judged is ingrained within us.
Very universal.

Carl Jung used to say that we have a personalized subconscious mind & a universal subconscious mind. The personal subconscious mind is catered towards our own experiences. But the universal one?
It's the one that mankind shares.

I often found it spooky when I thought I made a miraculous insight to only see some random person from 500 years ago made the same exact insight. How?
It's because of the universality that our singularity rests upon.

Times change...

The same ancestors who passed us the fear of being judged
were the ones who had a legitimate fear. They would be
killed if they were ostracized by their tribe. But in today's
era, things are different.

We can communicate via words, have houses, refrigerators
etc. All the stuff that our ancient ancestors did not have.

If they were teleported to this era, where they didn't
have to worry about being chased by a tiger, they would
ask:
'Why the fuck do you care about opinions for? Just chill!'

That's not to say that someone shouldn't display decorum or
responsibility. Having an awareness towards other people's
opinions allows a person to take feedback and serve as a
functioning member of society.

It's the serial killers who don't care at all. Which is not good.

The fat cat was chill because it took life day by day.
It does not have the advanced thinking faculties of the
human.

The unique path in life is the road less taken.
There is poetry in it.

The road less taken is more fulfilling when it's created after
introspection and insight. Being different for the sake of
being different is the same as trying to fit in.

2 sides of the same coin.

Being different as a byproduct of being you is where you
get fulfillment.

I once had a speaking mentor who was trying to tell me not
to curse at all during my YouTube videos and to talk about
topics which were only public speaking related. But that
just wasn't me.

Mentors can be a big liability at times.
People don't talk about that.

The world is your mentor.
The only real exclusive mentor for us is our future self.

It's the guardian angel who has been looking over us our
entire life, lovingly. Hoping we listen.

The logical brain tunes it out.
The logical brain thrives of making sure it's not judged.

When thinking is turned down, the fat cat is unlocked.

That's when you can hear your future self telling you what
you have known your entire life. It will feel like an insight.

Another part of it will feel like a lifelong truth.

THE SECRET LANGUAGE EVERYONE KNOWS

When I was a new engineer at one of my companies, a lot of the Operations managers would request I attend the meetings. The older engineers were confused.

Why were the managers asking this junior to attend while there were so many seniors capable of relaying the message? I was confused myself.

So one day, I decided to ask.

The manager's name was Debra. I asked Debra why she asked me to attend these meetings and not the other senior engineers?

She responded with:
'Because you talk in a way where we can understand.'
Aha!

The senior engineers were a little **TOO** qualified. They were so qualified to a point where they would accidentally speak a foreign language.

'The circuitry for the capacitor has drainage fluid which will require a new restoration template blah blah blah.'

In the world of the senior managers, they were simply relaying the information. For the Operations team, they heard a whole bunch of mumbo jumbo.

We all speak a secret language.

Typically, this language is a passion or something we do for
a living.

- o   When I hear a plumber talk about their profession,
      they use words I've never heard of in my life.
- o   When I hear a Facebook ads expert talk, they often
      drop concepts which are new to me.
- o   When I hear a chef describe a certain dish.... well,
      you get the point.

Learning a skill isn't just learning a skill.
In many ways, *it alters us as a person.*

If we are not careful, this can be a bad thing.
'A bad thing how?'
We may make the social sin of being overly complicated
with our delivery.

Just because it's easy for us to understand does not mean
it's easy for the other person to understand. Realize this...

The person you are speaking to may have no clue about the
details of your profession. Nor may they have the same
passion.

This is why analogies keep it simple.

One should not talk in a way to prove how smart they are
in a field. More often than not, the other person does not
care.
They just care about comprehension.

Which is why most of my stories are written in a way where a 4-year-old can understand it. I don't do this to only dumb myself down.

I do this to exercise my simplification muscle.

In the world of communication:
- o   The great communicators turn complex subjects into simple ones.
- o   The bad communicators turn simple subjects into complex ones.

This is why I follow the mantra:
Get to the point.

It's great to learn the secret language of a skill set.
Kudos.

It's even more great to allow someone else to understand it as well. Each time you relay your message effectively, each time you will melt away complexities in the conversation. This allows for a fluid dialogue.

The next time you catch yourself being too detailed, check yo' self!

Then remember the 4 golden words:
Get to the point.

Your conversation partner will thank you.

PUNK'D

I was scrolling through YouTube and I see a clip titled:
"MTV archives."
Something like that.

It was hard to tell what the video was about based on the
thumbnail. So, I decided to click on it.

Once the video started, I could tell exactly what it was.
It was a throwback episode of Punk'D.
When Ashton Kutcher was the host.

That was the OG era of the show.
Extremely entertaining.

If you never heard of the show, let me just give a quick
description.
  o *Ashton Kutcher, the host, sets up pranks on famous*
     celebrities.

A lot of the pranks were outrageous.
The funny part was the celebrity reactions.
It was unrehearsed & raw footage.

As I was watching the show, it took me down memory
lane.
This was the era before social media.

Yet, this show had a social media vibe to it.
Quick cut scenes.
Brash humor.

Pranking.

This wasn't normal at that time.
Punk'd was a show that was ahead of its time.

Also, the show proved how versatile Ashton Kutcher was
as a creator. At that point, he proved himself to be a
successful sitcom actor, movie actor and a hit television
show producer.

It may seem like a blasphemous claim...
But Punk'd had a similar effect as the Chappelle Show to
culture.

'What?? Are you kidding me?! Nothing can touch the
Chappelle show!'
No, you're missing my point.

*What I mean by similar effects is the ripples that it created for
the entertainment industry.*

Because of Chappelle, we had other sketch comedy shows
that began to erupt. Mind of Mencia was popping in 2005.
Key & Peele took off as well.

Because of Ashton Kutcher, prank shows became lit. A lot
of these pranksters took their talents to YouTube.
Nowadays, there are tons of prank channels on the web.

Chappelle's talent spilled over to the digital age as well,
now that I think about it. There are people banking from
doing Instagram skits. King Bach is an example.

The show Punk'd is a show that can teach you a lot about human nature.
This is a show that displays natural reactions of surprise, anger & fear.

I found it unique that the show exists even nowadays, especially with how everything is politically correct.
'You shouldn't prank! That may hurt someone's feelings.'

Last I checked, I think the host was Justin Bieber or Miley Cyrus for the new era. Nothing against them. But the Ashton Kutcher Punk'd is what I consider the golden era of the show.

Throwback entertainment is a great way to keep your creativity radiating.

The concept of running out of ideas seem laughable.
How can we run out?
Great ideas are all around us.

THERE'S ALWAYS SOMEONE "BETTER"

Did you ever date someone who worried a lot? It's like you were constantly having to give them a pep talk.

I used to have this self-conscious girlfriend.
She was always worried about what others thought of her.

Despite the worries, she was incredibly talented.
Let's call her Stacy.

Stacy was a great singer. However, she didn't believe she was a great singer. Would always doubt her abilities.

One day, I went to pick her up for lunch. When I walked into her place, I saw her singing this song. She was recording it on her phone. It was really good.

Once she saw me walk in, she got really embarrassed & put the phone away.

I told her it was good. To take it a level further, I told her she should upload the recording to Facebook! A lot of people would be amazed by her talent.

But like I said, she was self-conscious. Talking about how she couldn't do it. Even though you could tell she needed a bit more nudging.

Eventually, she decided to pull the trigger.

She uploaded that video on Facebook.
The video was doing well with engagement.

Then suddenly, something happened...

Julia, one of our other friends uploaded a video of her singing as well. She ended up releasing the video at the same exact time.

Not going to lie, Julia was **REALLLY, REALLY, REALLY** good.
She was flawless. A voice from the heavens.

When Stacy saw this, she started crying & felt like she "lost."
Even though her video was good, she started comparing herself to Julia and that's when hell ensued.

I wanted to hold in my laughter.
Pretty bad of me to say.
But it was too funny.

The timing of the whole thing was so peculiar.
It's like nature was trying to teach me a lesson.
Especially considering that Julia rarely posted.

However, on this particular day, she wanted to post??
And it just happened to be a singing video??
At the same exact time??
Yea, nature was trying to teach me a lesson.

The thing is, there is always someone better than us at something. No matter where the talent level is.

I saw an interview of Will Smith a while back in the
Breakfast Club where he said that he was getting jealous of
The Rock. He was getting jealous because The Rock was
stacking up more blockbuster hits than him.

Will Smith isn't some sort of D list celebrity. He's a big
star too. But in the comparison of numbers, The Rock was
winning.

I wonder if The Rock feels a few steps behind someone as
well. He also has had a lot of problems in his life too.

There was a speech he gave in the Laker's locker-room a
few years back where he talked about being a massive
failure in his past. The memories of darkness still haunts
him to this day. The haunting memories is what inspires
him to be great.

Point is, when you level up enough, there is always
someone better in one aspect of life. And the untamed
mindset can create the incorrect narrative out of that.

You compare yourself to what they are like now. But you
don't know the training they got beforehand.

I have no clue how Julia got so good. I think her mom was
a singer. Saw a few pictures of her mom singing in different
weddings. Julia probably learned early on.

The comparison game gets some people motivated to do
better. That seems like training wheels for development,
not riding the bike without the training wheels.

It's sort of like thinking in vibrations. When you know a field very well, you go past the words alone.

When you really know a field, you realize that the words were just training wheels for the mind to grasp hold of concepts.

Once you begin getting in your groove, the words can take the back burner, and now pictures & vibrations become royal.

Well, with comparing yourself to others, it's the same thing. That may start off your journey. But if that's all that is keeping you motivated, then you never grow.

In Wallace Wattles book, Science of Getting Rich, he talks about **2** ways of creating wealth.
-The competitive way.
-The creator's way.

He talks about how the competition method is from a lower form of consciousness. Where someone has to lose for you to win.

Can you build wealth this way? Sure. But that's not the way he recommends.

He talks about raising your consciousness to the creator's mindset. Where no one loses when you win.

An example of a creator's mindset is this book.

If my reader gets more value from this book than the amount paid, then no one had to lose for me to get a win.

That's the paradigm Wallace is urging people to evolve into.

Comparisons strip away creativity because it conditions the mind to follow too many other people. Eventually, your desires begin to rule you.

Remember this:
-Too many desires make you emotional.
-Few desires spark movement.
-1 gargantuan desire creates a legacy.

Combining all your desires into one big monster desire makes you a creative assassin. Comparing yourself to others becomes laughable because no one is fully doing something that you are wanting to do.

It's good to keep that desire to yourself.

When you created that one big monster desire, you may want to announce it to everyone. But why?

I know why.
It's the same roots of the competitor mindset creeping in.
You want some sort of approval.

All in all, becoming a creator is much harder than becoming a competitor.
- o It's easy to see a person like Julia and be like, *"damn, I am really behind."*
- o It's another thing to see a Julia & say, *"I respect what she is capable of doing."*
Then you go back to taking care of business.

Different paradigms lead to different moves.
This book is all about pushing the creator's mindset.

I do believe competition has a special spot in this world.
But only if you are using it as a steppingstone to reach
something greater.

WHAT ALL LEADERS SHOULD KNOW

Most individuals have to take up a leadership role at one point or another in their lives.
- o Leading a group project at school because everyone in the team is lazy.
- o Leading a group project at work.
- o Parenting.

In all cases, we are discussing people.
What is a great way to spark people into action?

It's to speak to their intangibles.
Let me share what that means.

My first ever job was in a Subway restaurant.
It's good to work in fast food in my opinion.
Great way to build thick skin.

I saw this firsthand when my manager once got a bunch of coins thrown at his face and all he could do was apologize.

The Subway I worked in was the one at the mall. More specifically, the food court. The mall Subways didn't run the 5-dollar footlong deal on all their subs.

When I was working in Subway around 2007ish, that's when the whole:
"5-dollar....5-dollar...5-dollar footlong" jingle was popping!
This jingle made Subway relevant again.

Most Subways were running the 5-dollar footlong deal for
all their subs. But the Subways in the mall?
The deal only applied to a select few subs.

One day, this lady ordered the Italian BMT. Once she was
told it wasn't a part of the 5-dollar footlong deal, she
was irate. She felt like she was lied to.

My manager's name was Ashish.

Ashish tried explaining that the Subway's in the mall
follow different rules, but she wasn't having it. She
begrudgingly pulled out the extra coins from her purse &
threw it in Ashish's face.

I thought he was going to yell back. But nope, all he did
was apologize.

Ashish's life was Subway.

He would work 11 hours every day. I mean every day. 7
days a week. He expected his employees to have the same
hustler's attitude.

Overall, Ashish was an awful manager. Wouldn't give us
breaks and would have us working nonstop.

During the time, the minimum wage was 6.79$. Well,
when Florida passed a new minimum wage from 6.79$ to
7.21$... Ashish tried to play it off like he was giving us a
raise!
The man was a piece of shit.

But he always got the most out of his workers. Any idea why?
'No, why?'
Because he referred to us as *Sandwich Artists.*

When I first started Subway, I viewed the job as the guy who just made subs. A very bland title.

However, when the employees got started, Ashish would drill into our minds that we were Sandwich Artists.

Just hearing that title made us more motivated. Like we were contributing to something bigger.

One day, Ashish decides to take off early. The mall was empty, so he thought I would be good by myself until closing.

Around that time, there was a lady that came up & ordered a roast beef sub. As I was making her sub, she began speaking to me:
'Hey there young man, you are making the sub look very good! I love how you are evenly spreading out everything. Keep going! A big tip is on your way.'

A big tip? You think I'm making the sub look very good? Okay, I will keep going!
This is what I thought.

Once I was done, she gave me a 5-dollar tip. Which was a lot to a high school kid.

Wait a minute...

This was **2** times this happened. Someone made me feel like an artist, and it was a great feeling.

Despite Ashish being a bad boss, he got the most out of his workers because he made them feel bigger in their position.

If a leader can make their talent feel like the artist of their field, then they will have better talent.
- o   Praise someone's skill to speak to their head.
- o   Praise someone's work ethic to speak to their heart.

The beauty about making someone feel like an artist is that it speaks to their head and heart.

An artist is defined as a very <u>skilled</u> individual in a certain craft. How do you get skilled? Through <u>work ethic</u>.

Even today, if you go to a Subway, tell the sandwich maker that they are a Sandwich Artist. You'll notice how their mannerisms change.

I came to learn that Ashish was not the only Subway to do the whole Sandwich Artist thing. Apparently, all Subways do that. But only a few of the mangers really emphasized it.

When I was in high school, any job experience was good experience. I was happy to be getting out of the house to work.

However, in plenty of occasions, a lot of people we hire, whether for small projects or big projects, are not happy with their jobs. They mainly do it to pay their bills.

By capturing their narrative mind, we can engage them.

That's not to say that poor work should be tolerated.

But if they are good, engage their artistic side, to make them great.

A combination of praising skills & work ethic refines a person's movements. It allows them to feel bigger than the field that they are occupying.

What is the byproduct of an organism being larger than their present property?
They are bound to evolve.

From animals gaining new body parts to humans gaining deeper mental faculties.

A leader allows those around them to evolve. Turn them from doing a job to producing art, and you will rarely have difficulty finding talent.

THE LANGUAGE OF MONEY

Picture you're in a restaurant with a few friends and you're getting ready to order something. This is a new restaurant, so the menu looks a little fuzzy. Everything sounds good! *Choices.*

Eventually, you decide on your order and your friends decide on theirs. The waitress comes & takes the orders.

After 20 minutes or so, the food is arriving. Everything smells good.

The waitress is individually giving everyone their plates. You look along eagerly waiting for your dish.

By the time all the dishes come, you make a sad realization. 'What's that?' You didn't get as much food as the others.

Your friends ordered the dishes that gave a lot of food. But your dish? Eh.

You're able to swallow this one though. It's because everyone ordered DIFFERENT dishes.

But imagine if everyone ordered the same dish.

Everyone got a lot of food, but you got a little. How would you feel?

'I would feel livid!'
Why?
'It's because it's not fair. I ordered the same dish. How come mine is so little?'

Feel that level of anger. That's the anger we feel when we feel like something unfair happened.

This is a tricky situation to be in, no?
Because what is fair & what is unfair?

If we are using ourselves as a component to measure fair/unfair, immediately we introduce the gray world of humans. Things get tricky.

This can get even trickier as society scales. Therefore, it's imperative that we have units that allow us to circumnavigate this unfair issue.

This is how language comes to be.
An agreement that allows us to comprehend messages.

That's what money comes down to as well.
An agreement.

If someone were to ask you, can you explain money to me?
And your explanation needs to include an analogy, would you be able to do it?

I can do it with an old man and a hooker.
'For real??'
Yes. Let me illustrate money being an agreement with the following analogy.

Paul has been married to his high school sweetheart for 20 years. He is in his 50s, has kids & is ready to keep his life the way it is.

Until suddenly, his wife divorces him & leaves him for a younger man. His kids are now in college. *Suddenly, Paul is lonely.*

Months go by. Paul is sad. To make the situation worse, Paul hasn't gotten laid in a hot minute. He's starting to get desperate.

It just so happens that one of Paul's friend's is also divorced & is aware of hookers around the area. He gives Paul a connection.

Now Paul is about to call on the hooker & get a deal going.
How can they momentarily speak the same language?

-Paul wants sex.
-The hooker wants money.

Sex is the perceived valuable service.
Money serves as the AGREEMENT to make the transaction occur.

To understand the depth of this example, hypothetically picture that Paul and this hooker were introduced in different circumstances. Let's say they go to the same networking event. The hooker is in her mid-20s. Paul is in his mid-50s.

What other commonalities do they have? Other than speaking English, what other languages can they speak in order to connect? Football, music, hobbies?? What else is there?

When we start to look at it like this, the concept of money allowed 2 different personalities to temporarily connect. So yes, money is an agreement.

I worked with a client a few months back who said that he needed to find the fine balance between giving & taking. His problem was that his leadership style kept causing others to become lazy. Others were treating him like a doormat.

That's because his leadership style was in terms of the GIVER rather than the person who conducts AGREEMENTS.
'What's the difference?'
Agreements also place importance on us as well.

Too much emphasis is placed on giving while not much emphasis is placed on taking. Humans like to be taken from too, as counterproductive as it sounds.

It's our material nature to take as well. No shame in the game. That's why consumption is even a thing. Even our body naturally gets hungry.

Conducting agreements not only gets you to place some damn importance on yourself, but it also prevents you from being a scumbag.

This mindset allows us to become more narrative focused as well. Every human has a narrative & perception that leads to their behavior. When we focus on agreements, we can view my hooker example from a different light.

Because if you've been paying attention, I said that money is an agreement. Paul got his sex. The hooker, Stacy, got her money.
'Ah, she has a name.'
Yes, she has a name. The analogy is now going from 2D -> 3D.

Is Stacy only looking for money?
No.
What is Stacy using that money for?
To pay rent.
To buy food.
To survive.

We initially saw money, but when we delve deeper, we can view the money from the context of her experience.
Through the context of her narrative mind.

Hopefully, you see what I am trying to say.
This is why anything becomes communication when viewed from the right perspective.

Making communication the centerpiece of a business allows us to conduct ethical business practices while *we* win as well.

Money was never the root of all evil.
Lack of money was the root of all evil.

But what is even more sad is the lack of knowledge, the lack of perception, and the lack of language regarding money.
That is the worst of them all.

When viewing the world through the elegant lens of communication, random occurrences of the world suddenly begin to make much more sense.

LIFE WAS NEVER FAIR

February 9th, 2014. One of the saddest days of my life. Who am I kidding? It was one of the saddest days of the community's life.

'What happened?'

I will tell you about that day. But first, I have to tell you about February 8th, 2014.

FEBRUARY 8TH

It was a normal day. I just parked on campus and was running late for my group meeting.

Out of nowhere, I see a close friend who I had not seen in a while. We wave hi to each other. I was very tempted to stay back and have a conversation with him.

I hadn't seen my friend in a while. But I was late. Oh well, I will go ahead and give him a call later.

MAKE UP TIME

I texted my friend to let him know that I was sorry for running off. I invited him to have lunch whenever he was free.

'Sure bro. By the way, we are all going out tonight. The squad bro. Let's turn up,' said my friend.

The squad consisted of 3 other friends. We were all close.

But sometimes, life gets busy, you know? The group had not been as close for some time.

However, we were the type of squad that could get back together after months and pick up right where we left off. We were always brothers.

'You know what? I will take you up on that offer,' I said. It was bound to be a lit ass night.

NOT SO FAST

My buzzkillington group member for a project came to me and broke some news.

'Not sure if you know this Armani. But we are meeting up at 8 am tomorrow. We are behind, and need this meeting to get work done,' said the member in a sharp tone.

Lame as fuck.

Oh well, I guess I have to cancel on the plans tonight. I text my friend to let him know what was up.

'Haha that sucks man. Okay, I'll let the other 3 know. Goodluck getting up early' texted my friend.

And that was all.
Went to bed at 9 pm that night.
Set the alarm.
Lights off.
Zzzz....

FEBRUARY 9TH

My brother knocks on my door. I was supposed to be up early, why is he knocking?

He comes in.
He has a somber face.

'Hey, listen. I don't know how to tell you this. But your friends got in a car accident last night. They were all killed by a drunk driver.'

Silence

The crippling pain began to manifest within me.
No no no...
This isn't real.
Please don't let this be real.
There is no way this could have happened.
What the fuck? They were such good fuckin people. They were....

ANGELS. They were just about to graduate college. They had yet to live their best life. They had siblings. They had a mom and dad. They had friends. They had a family. They had interests and hobbies. They had dreams and goals. They bled the same blood as us. They took in the same air as we did. They were human. This isn't fair. Why the fuck did that guy have to get behind the wheel drunk? Why wasn't that dumbass more responsible?

My friends didn't deserve to die.
They were all such good fucking people.
4 high character angels that wouldn't harm a fly.

Why them?

I feel so much pain. I feel so numb. I can't move. I want to change what happened. This can't be real. This has to be a nightmare.
Why them?

PRESENT

I still ask myself that same question.
Why them?
Why do angels get killed by demons?

It is not fair.
I learned something that night. Life is not fair.

I see it daily.
Innocent people who died too soon.

My 4 friends taught me something that night, life was never fair.

I knew them very well. They were the type of people who would want their family and friends to remember their great memories and carry out life with honor.

That is exactly what I plan to do.

I will embody the character of the 4 angels for the rest of my life. I know you guys are watching, and I will not let you all down.

Mark my words.

WHAT DID YOU LEARN FROM THIS?

One, before complaining and whining, ask yourself the following:

- Can I tackle this situation?
- Can this conflict help me grow and gain wisdom down the line?
- Does whining serve me any purpose or can I use my energy more efficiently?

You will always get stronger and stronger. The lessons learned and wisdom gained will put you light years ahead of your progress if you always learn from your conflicts.

Two, understand that your loved ones are important. I still regret not being a few minutes late to my group meeting.

I wish life had a do-over button.
Look, I get it. You want to build your empire.
But listen carefully when I say this.

You know when you are on your death bed? You will not give a fuck about the money, the cars and the followers.

You will look back at the chapters of your life and remember your loved ones and your unique experiences. That is what really is important.

The time is now.

There are 168 hours in the week. You can allocate at least 3-4 hours to catch up with your close friends and family.

Human beings are way more important than material possessions.

NOT EVEN CLOSE.

You can always get another item. But you can never give life back to someone when they have taken their last breath.

Life was never fair.
So maintain strong relationships with your loved ones at all times.

Do not be the person who regrets not making that phone call a bit sooner.

SPEED READING

An underrated skill is speed reading. The art of reading fast
while maintaining comprehension.

A while back, I used to be an awful reader. I didn't have
much comprehension behind the words. My goal was to get
through it & give myself a pat on the back.

But when I was done?
I had o clue on what I read.

Spent years thinking that it was either speed reading OR
comprehension. But it couldn't do both.
'Were you right?'
Nope, I was wrong.

I discovered the error in my ways when I lived in Virginia
and was riding in the Metro. There was this guy sitting
next to me who was looking intently at his phone.

Chinese man with glasses, a big pair of headphones on &
a serious face. His eyes were glued to his phone.

This was a late party night in Virginia where a bunch of
drunk people were bumping along his shoulders and legs as
they tried to wobble their way to their seats.

But his focus did not waver.

ONE. WORD. AT. A. TIME. WAS. FLASHING.
ON. HIS. PHONE.

He was just looking at it.

Something about this seemed peculiar. Why is he reading one word at a time? Where are the sentences?

After a while, curiosity got the best of me & I tapped him on the shoulder.

He paused his game, took off his headphones and his super serious face turned gentle. 'Whatsup homie?' he asked. I asked him what he had going on in his phone.

He said he was practicing speed reading. His approach was unique.

Rather than speed reading entire sentences, he took it one word at a time.

Just type 'speed reading' in the app section of your phone & you'll see plenty of apps which get recommended. Most of them have an approach to flash one word at a time to get you started.

Once you learn how to read the flashing words, then the game evolves. Now it's a matter of moving your eyes from left to right. This requires motor sensory skills, so don't rush it. Practice it slowly.

Left to right.
Left to right.
Left to right.

What happens all too often is that we get fixated on one word. When we get fixated, we lose comprehension.

Just keep practicing the left to right movement.

Over time, this speed-reading exercise turns into a workout for the mind. It becomes easier to read faster and maintain comprehension.

This is a great skill to invest in because we are inundated with words all day. Practice opportunities are staring anywhere we look.

And let's keep it real.
Reading a book takes time.
Time that you will never get back.

If you like spending your time reading a book, then go for it.
But for me, I have other stuff to do.

Speed reading, it is.

HOW TO MAINTAIN YOUR COOL

Every now and then, I check out the Uber Eats app when I am feeling lazy or am busy. I use them at night, never the day. The Uber Eats app is clutch, because the area I live in has a lot of great food spots.

However, my last 3 experiences with Uber Eats have been annoying.

Nothing against the food.
Rather, the delivery.

The first time, it was an elderly lady delivering to my crib. Her name was Susan.

By the time she got here, she couldn't find my place. So, she called.

'I think you gave me the wrong address,' she said.
No, I gave you the address that the food is always delivered to.
'Uh, okay. Mind staying on the phone with me till I find it?' she asked.

She was in who knows where. After 35 minutes on the phone with her, she finally found my apartment.

That was an out of ordinary experience.
If I wanted to wait 35 minutes, then I would of just drove and picked up the food myself.
All good.

Strike 1.

The second time, my order pickup time kept getting pushed
back.

Pushed back 5 minutes.
20 minutes.
35 minutes.
1 HOUR.

Then the order suddenly gets cancelled.
Tsk tsk.
1 hour I'll never get back.

For the 3rd time, I was entering with an irritated attitude.
I wanted to make sure no fuckups happened. Just drop my
food off at the door & that's it. Will this be possible?

Well, Steve was my delivery driver. How would he face
the pressure that my imagination had set for him?

Like a bum.

Steve was 30 minutes late and he wasn't answering my
calls back. By the time he did arrive, I was ready to yell at
him. To give him a piece of my mind.

He asked me to meet him at his car, because he was
disabled and wasn't feeling well. As I walked on over to his
car, I saw him. And made eye contact with the guy.

*A 70-year-old man, who had a cane & was doing the best he
could.*

As we made eye contact, my anger dissipated. I got my
food, thanked him, and went back to my apartment.

There's a big hack I learned in regard to anger.
If you make eye contact with the person who you are about
to lose your cool with, you become more composed.

Not always.
Sometimes the act was so bad that you still feel rage.

But a lot of times, composure kicks in. The eye contact
humanizes the person & it's easier to evaluate them as a
person rather than their mistake.

This is the reason why it's easy to talk shit behind the
screens. The hater never makes eye contact with the
person. That's why the same people who have balls behind
the screen are meek when you meet them. They don't have
that same tone.

The eyes speak volumes.

The awesome part is that physical contact does not need to
be made. Someone's eyes can speak a language on its own.
It's the language of the subconscious mind.

This is just a hack.

The bigger lesson is to keep the eyes on the bigger picture.
A temper tantrum feels good while you are doing it. But
after you are done, you feel embarrassed.

An ill-timed temper tantrum can ruin everything you
worked for and you have to rebuild all over.

It's annoying.
Not worth the hassle.

This is coming from someone who has had his fair share of
temper tantrums.
We all have them.

Now it's a game of lowering our entropy and finding out
what works to keep us more composed. Thick skin is built
when a temper tantrum is second guessed.

During that second guessing process of:
'Is the tantrum worth it?'
  o   Judgment builds.
  o   Thick skin builds.
  o   Composure builds.

The thicker the skin, the less the stress.

People are always going to have irritating habits about
them. Can't control that. What you can control is you.

Slow down, silence the breath, look into the eyes & pick
the next moves wisely.

BECOMING A BEGINNER AGAIN

I used to have a YouTube channel in college for one of my classes.

Once we were done with our projects, we needed to make a video to share with our class. My old YouTube channel had 3 videos.

As I was watching it, a part of me got curious about video editing. A great editor can turn raw boring footage into a story full of life.

After discovering my old YouTube channel, I decided to learn some video editing for my ArmaniTalks YouTube channel.

Since learning video editing, it's been a bumpy ride.

From finding the right software, looking for the right music, and dealing with software crashes. It's been a zig zagging process.

Learning something new is always bumpy.

The annoying part is that in the beginning, the newbie is the most enthusiastic. This newbie wants the enthusiasm to produce practical results! Not have it wasted on the little details.

However, being a beginner again teaches the art of humbling oneself.

As I continued editing the video clips, I saw how awful my final product looked.
By awful, I mean terribly awful. My enthusiasm waned as I saw other video editors doing their magic. Even though their progress discouraged me because it showed how far I was from the target, it also gave me hope.

This talk is not about video editing. It's about learning the art of discovering how to become a beginner again.

One of the massive insights that I learned from being a beginner again with video editing was:
How much I appreciate good teachers.

There have been a bunch of videos where the teachers are awful & use too many fancy phrases.

I discovered 1 guy who has an awkward personality. Fidgety guy who seems a little geeky. But he speaks in a simple way that I can understand. So, I listen.

Great teachers make a beginner's life easier. Being a beginner again gives the student real life lessons on how to be a meaningful teacher in the future.

Are you a beginner again?
If not now, one day, you may be.

When that time comes, keep enjoying the process.
Especially when it feels like your enthusiasm is waning.

DO YOU TRY TO ONE UP OTHERS?

The lines above are the lines of one of my most viral tweets. I wrote it after a meeting. Then my phone died on the car ride back home.

Once I got home, I saw how many people were commenting on it & quote retweeting about it.

They were saying stuff like:
-FACTS!!
-This is so true! I need to work on this.
-Some people just need to shut up & listen.

So many people agreeing with this.

This was one of my first moments when a tweet had gone semi-viral, and for the most part, everyone was in general agreement.

There were no fractions arguing with each other.
Why?

Because this tweet represented a common problem that everyone faces...

It's a common mistake that we can make when hearing the wins of others.

-We believe their win signifies our loss.
OR
-We want to relate to the win somehow. So, we bring ourselves up & forget the initial win the other person was talking about.

A moment like that happened to me when I first monetized my YouTube account. That's when I could start showing ads on all my videos. This was great news for me and a massive win because a lot of the hard work was now showing fruits.

One of my friends who also had a YouTube channel called me. I told him about the monetization of my channel.

And he goes like:
'Congrats bro. I'm pretty sure I'll be there soon as well. And here's why....'

This friend starts yapping away for the next 20 minutes.

I've known him for over 8 years. Overall, he is a good guy. Not a malicious guy by any means. However, it goes to show that this is a universal mistake. We may try to show up others consciously or subconsciously.

What's the fix for this?
Talk less when someone wins & let them talk more.

The tweet went viral because it's a widespread problem. Faced by good people & annoying people. It's something that our ego wants to do when others win.

In my opinion, this is why it's good to go through a phase where you were shy or socially awkward. You are more sensitive to spotting when you are over talking in a dialogue.

People who talk too much or are too competitive will find the act of talking less when someone wins to be highly difficult.

To them:
1. It feels like they are 'losing.'
2. Or they feel that immediately contributing their own win is the smart social move.

No and no.

Just shut up & let the other person have the spotlight. This is the easiest way to build charisma. The stage is already set.

The other person has won. So, there is positive energy in the field.

They are interacting with you. So, there is an opportunity for the person to tie that positive energy to you. Just like that, the rapport has been deepened.

However, if you make this moment about you, then you have:
1. Disrupted the positive energy.
2. Created negative energy.

3. The other person associates the negative energy to you.

Most interactions are guiding us towards knowing when to speak & when not to speak.

Be aware of being the person who makes everything about themself. Not a good look at all.

WHY EVERYTHING HAS A PRICE

There was a day when I was watching a TV show of a professional athlete who was enjoying his day.

Then randomly...
He found out that he got traded by his sports team.

As he was hearing the news, it sounded like his wife said:
'Do you feel betrayed?'

However, I misheard.

She actually said:
'Did you know you would be traded?'

-Betrayed
-Be traded
The two sound so similar.

When you looked at that athlete's face, he definitely looked betrayed.

He knew that now he had to move his family to a new location, build chemistry with a brand-new team & shake up his life. Just like that.

The athletic profession is glorified in the world. When we look at athletes, we think these are people who have everything figured out.

Millions of dollars, fans, and they get paid to play the sport of their dreams. Yet, even these people are subject to betrayal.

When I was in the 12th grade, YouTube was getting bigger.
Every now and then, I would watch videos of celebrities dealing with the paparazzi.

There was a bizarre video I once saw of Paris Hilton getting swarmed by the paparazzi.

I knew Paris Hilton as someone who loved attention & loved the cameras being on her. However, this particular video was different.

She seemed to be under the weather & wanted some space. However, the paparazzi didn't want to give her that. They were asking her a bunch of questions & getting in her space.
You could tell that she was visibly upset.

She said, 'I'll answer your questions when I feel better.'

I don't know how she had that kind of patience. Better yet, I don't know how paparazzi's are even allowed. Some of those videos my 12th grade self saw looked like straight up harassment.

I would be tempted to punch them on the face & beat them over their head with the camera.

How do celebrities do that?
Better yet, do they really enjoy the paparazzi?

I'm sure some do.
They love the attention.

However, I believe a lot of them are lowkey.
They just want to be gifted at their skillset of choice &
then mind their own business.

This is what I love about new media. Targeted exposure.

PewDiePie is a success on YouTube with over 100 million
subscribers. However, if he walked into the mall, I doubt
everyone would recognize him. Only a certain fragment of
people would know that it was PewDiePie.

New media is much different than the cult like broad range
wierdo fans the old media created.

I bring up the sports athlete & Paris Hilton because it
shows how every profession has the dark sides.
The dark sides that people do not see.

In moments like this, I have no clue how you can push
yourself through it if you don't have love for the activity.

Imagine if that sports star who got trade was just naturally
gifted at the sport, but he never had any passion for the
game.

If he got traded once, he would probably be fine. On the
other hand, if he got traded 6 times in his career (which
happens to a lot of professional athletes) then he may have
been fuming.

Angry enough to quit.

That's why going in with the expectation that every field has a dark side/s is a must. Which is why passion, love & fun are variables that need to be weighed in.

It's one thing if the act is at a small scale. Let's say you are doing your first job in Dunkin Donuts. You may not have to love the job that much.

But still.
Even then, it's good if you can find a way to spark some love for it in a creative way.

This is coming from a guy who worked in Dunkin Donuts in college during the busiest times of 5am - 12pm.
'How did you make it fun?'
By telling myself that I was building thick skin dealing with these entitled customers.

Anything can turn into a learning opportunity.

It becomes easier when you have a vision. That's when random things which normally didn't make much sense, plug right in. There is no field out there without grunt work.

None at all.
Athletes & celebrities are not exempt either.

The goal is to just understand what price you are willing to pay. Because everything has a price.

The universe was designed in an interconnected manner.

From the air we breathe to the food we eat. You can cheat the system for so long. However, it's always learned the hard way, that there is no such thing as a free meal.

WORKING WHILE YOU'RE SAD

When I'm having a long day & don't want to think, I enjoy watching prank content. That's a way for me to unwind.

There was a day when I saw a popular prank channel post an update video about the status of their channel. This channel is composed of 2 people who play pranks on others and they are hilarious.

Well, one of the members was on the update video and looked pretty bummed out. He had sad news.

The sad news was that his partner decided to no longer do the videos.

This was sad news considering how the two were such a deadly duo. Why did the other person suddenly stop?

The person giving the update news was giving the audience an update of what it was like being a prank channel in year 2020. The year of a global pandemic.

He talked about the stress of being consistent and how difficult it was to work while sad. But him & his partner were trying their best. Well, the burnout finally caught up to his partner and now the channel has 1 member.

This got me thinking:
- o How should one work when they are sad?

What this got me thinking about even more was the difference between physical work & mental work.

When I'm sick for example, I've always been one of those people who could still do physical work if need be. I could still get up & move things around. Heck, sometimes when I'm sick, I go for a walk.

In contrast, when I'm sick, I hate thinking. I just want my mind to be in Lala land.

This prank channel, what are they really?
They are content creators.
What do content creators do?
They think at scale.

Even though these people were not physically sick, they were emotionally drained. Being emotionally drained simulates similar feelings as being physically sick.

I can understand where the partner who dropped out, was coming from.

In a case like this, what do we do? How does someone remain consistent, especially if their line of work relies heavily on mental faculties?

I have 2 suggestions.

1. Have backup material.
Picture a tragedy can strike later tonight. Will you still have material to last until you get back up on your feet?

2. Train yourself to work through the pain.
The first suggestion seems reasonable.
The second suggestion seems whacky.

'Work through emotional pain? That does not seem like the emotionally intelligent thing to do, buddy!'
As a matter of a fact, it is.

Emotional Intelligence comes down to:
1. Self-awareness.
2. Self-motivation.
3. Empathy.
4. Emotional regulation.
5. Social skills.

The ability to work through pain tackles (2) self-motivation & (4) emotional regulation.

This is the reason I believe all entrepreneurs should take their EQ seriously. It's difficult to measure what we don't have exams for.

This is why emotional intelligence can only be measured by individuals who have #1 from the list.
Self-awareness.

Because the truth of the matter is that tough moments occur. For a couple of days, weeks, months, we may be sad. Incredibly sad to say the least.

And training the mind to immediately be like:
'Oh no! I'm sad. No work today!'
Will install poor habits.

Not saying we should always work through sadness.
However, at times, working through the sadness is
a skillset.

It's a workout for our emotional muscles.
Makes us tougher, stronger & harder to kill.

Working past inhibiting emotions is what creates a warrior.

Not saying the guy who dropped out of the prank channel
is not a warrior. There are a lot of different reasons for why
& how a decision is made.

However, I know for me, working past sadness has led to
many of my happiest moments.

Take pride in consistency.
Consistency isn't always sexy.

But when the consistent ones are gone, it is their presence
which will leave a dent in the universe.

CONSCIENCE VS INTUITION

Steven Spielberg once said a quote that resonated with me.

He said:
"Conscience is different than intuition. Conscience is loud while intuition is quiet. Conscience screams: here's what you should do. Intuition whispers: here's what you could do."

This quote was compelling because it allowed me to understand what an insight was.

Normally, when I'm working with clients, they want some sort of an insight from me to help their performance in a speech.

Also, when someone reads my books, they are looking for some sort of an insight regarding communication.

What's ironic was that after helping thousands of people with insights, I couldn't quite define what an insight was.

Insight is something that delves into the intangibles. The part of a human that you cannot see. But can an insight be turned into an art & science? Can an insight be turned into a craft?

The answer is yes.

And that's why Steven Spielberg's quote stuck out.

Intuition & insight are joined at the hip.

To turn insights into a science & art, we need to move out of our own way. We need to learn the art of not thinking.

Not thinking may sound tricky.
That's like me saying, 'don't think of an elephant.'
The first thing you'll do is think of an elephant.
The mind is slick like that.

My trick to not thinking is to observe ourselves when we are not thinking. When we are fully in the present.

Doesn't matter who you are, there are bursts in the day when you are fully present.
- When you see a baby laughing.
- When you pet a cat.
- When you laugh at a comedian.

All these moments are when we disengage thinking faculties and live in the present.

A study was shown a while back of the difference in brain states of a rapper who was reading off rhymes vs freestyling.

Reading off rhymes allowed them to show regular brain wave patterns. Nothing unusual.

But when they freestyled? The brain portion that relates to the 'sense of self' heavily reduced.
It's like they were entering another portal.

That's why I often encourage my readers to try impromptu speaking. Find a topic & don't prepare at all. Just start sharing a talk. This allows us to experience a life where we do not have to think while speaking.

A big lie is that all content needs to be planned. You do not need to plan content when you live what you speak. Impromptu speaking should be our baseline state.

However, due to the heavy doses of technology in our daily life, we strayed away from who we are.

Presence is the natural state.
Thinking is the altered state.

But if I tell that to the modern person, they'll laugh at me. They can clearly remember all the times they thought in the day. However, they can't remotely think of when they were present.

That's like a person who initially knew how to swim but then forgot. Let's call him Ralph.

When Ralph returned to the swimming pool years later, he learned how to swim on his back.

Sure, swimming on the back can work. But Ralph forgot how to swim with his chest facing the water.

He gets challenged by his swimmer friends to race. All the other swimmers blow out Ralph because they are swimming correctly. They aren't swimming on their back.

Sure, swimming on the back is fun occasionally.
However, that's not the baseline state.

Sure, thinking is fun occasionally.
However, that's not the baseline state.

The goal is to return home.
Join the present moment again.

Society does not encourage that though.
'Why not?'
Because living in the present makes it difficult to brainwash
a person.

A person who overthinks, is a volatile individual & is
perfectly primed for brainwashing.

To tap into intuition consistently & create insights like a
machine, we need the presence. The presence knows no
arrogance, over thinking & anxiety. It's a state of calmness.

That's the state we need.

Lowkey, everyone wants this state.
Only a few will work for it.

Just take your hand at impromptu speaking to experience
this state.
1. Find topics.
2. Tell stories.

2 steps.
2 steps to see if you want it bad enough.

Everyone wants this state.
Only a few, tiny, minuscule percentage of people will ever
work for it.

HOW ROCK BOTTOM CHANGES YOU....FOR THE BEST

A few years ago, I was going through my personal rock bottom moment. It was the year of **2017** & a lot of things were falling apart before my eyes.

To kick this story off, I was getting sued for **250,000$** by some dude from England.
'Huh??'
Yep.

I was doing virtual real estate (website brokerage) back then & one of my designers had used one of the pictures from an England guy's website. Since I was the website owner, I was the one who was going to be facing the consequences.

Next, I was ending it with a longtime girlfriend where the relationship had taken its course. It sucked because she was great. But she had minimal ambition & was holding me back.

But wait, there's more.

One day, while I was in my car devising ways out of this suing situation, I ended up getting into a bad car accident. My car was totaled & one of the guys I hit was thinking about pressing charges too.

After the car got totaled, it felt like the final straw in what
had been an awful couple of days. This led to my
performance at work & school to suffer.

It was a tough time that had me thinking if my life was
going to spiral down from there on out. 25 years old at the
time & thinking if this was it?

I went through a level of depression & felt like a big loser.

Rock bottom has a way of draining your energy, making
you lose zest for life & killing your ambition along the way.
I went through week after week feeling like all hope was
lost.

Poor sleep, loss of appetite & minimal desire to talk to others.

After a few weeks in, I realized that this feeling could not
have gotten any worse. The worse that could have
happened, had happened. I was in the depth of darkness &
there was no one to blame but myself. Therefore, it would
be no one's duty to pull me out, but myself.

It was time to take a new journey.
A journey to take care of unfinished business.

The next day, I called the guy who was suing me. Not
email or text... But call.

I had felt so much pain for the past few days, that I had a
strange level of confidence in my voice.

A level of, *the worst has happened, so you don't scare me.*

I told him **250**k was outrageous & I was not going to be paying that much. Did some research beforehand and realized his pictures were on an **RSS** feed, so he was the one who lacked due diligence.

This dude was a straight up wimp. Soft voice, stuttering & mumbling.

He sounded like a tough guy on email, but he was far from that on the phone.

He ended up dropping the charges & asked me to only pay **500**$ for lost money on his website.
Fine.

Next, I ended up having to wait out the aftermath of the accident. But within **2** weeks, my car was fixed & I had gotten a lot of my money reimbursed due to the insurance plan my family has.

After I had gotten my car back, it was time to play catch up at work & school. I stayed extra hours at work & busted my ass. Did extra projects, volunteered to work overtime & networked with others to get back on their good graces.

As for school, I would sacrifice my next couple of Fridays & weekends studying my ass off to finish the semester of with a bang.

Finally, I got my ass in the gym & joined a Toastmasters. Decided I was going to chronicle my whole journey out of darkness via Twitter. I didn't give a fuck about followers, more about sharing my message with the world.

That is how the ArmaniTalks page was born.

If you are someone going through a tough time right now, understand it is only a fraction of your life. It is not the final chapter, but rather chapter 1.

I thought my darkness would lead me to a spiral. But instead, it led me to my life meaning.

You learn more about yourself in the darkness than you do when things are going well.

You learn to endure pain, think creatively & find a greater joy for the smaller things in life. That is how rock-bottom changes you for the best.

Always hold your head up & show up. You will be tempted to throw in the towel & grovel like a bitch.

That is normal.
Go on & be sad if you need to. You are human at the end of the day.

But it is your duty to brush yourself off & get back out there. Go to the gym, pick up a hobby that keeps you creative & start a side hustle.

This was my formula for engineering my way out of rock bottom.

The sole goal of rock bottom is to level the fuck up.

We all have a second chance in this life.
It's called tomorrow.

THE TRUTH ABOUT LAW OF ATTRACTION

When I used to hear about the law of attraction, I thought it was a bunch of crap. You visualize something, work towards it & you will attract it?

That just sounds like hard work to me.

'When did your perspective regarding the topic change?' When I noticed its effects.

A few years ago, I was at a stage where I was starting an athletics wardrobe company.

It was a drop shipping company that I was investing a lot of my energy in.

Around that time, my engineering job had built a pathway behind our building where the workers could walk around to unwind & get active.

Every day, I began to walk around that pathway listening to very hype music that made me feel. Every time I was walking in that path, I was imagining a bunch of cool thoughts.

My thoughts were rarely about my athletics company. Rather, it was about public speaking.

I was on stage with hundreds of people watching me, and they were intrigued by what I was saying.

Day in & day out, my mind defaulted to these thoughts during the walks.

Eventually, I came to a point where I realized that public speaking may be calling my name.

So, I decided to start the ArmaniTalks Twitter page as a hobby. Plus, I was going through a tough time in my life. This would be a great creative outlet in addition to it being a hobby!

However, during that time, my gut ended up telling me that this page was going to be much bigger than a hobby.

I tweeted every day for 2 weeks straight & racked up a stunning 3 followers.

Seemed like no one really cared about public speaking. But oh well, I knew that this was just for fun.

For some strange reason, I still had this *feeling* that this page was going to be bigger.

3 weeks into tweeting every day, I told my friend that I would eventually have to make a choice. I would either have to invest my time towards my athletics company or ArmaniTalks. I had to choose.

He looked at me like I was crazy.
'Bro, you have 8 followers on your Twitter page. What makes you want to leave your athletics business for that?'

And he had a point.

I had nothing to show for my work. But deep inside, I had faith that something was going to happen.

Guess what?
In a few weeks, the faith had served its purpose.

One night, I turned down a party to do some writing.

That was the same night an account who went by the name, WesternMastery, found one of my tweets & decided to give me a shout out. Overnight, I got my big break & racked up 200 new followers.

This led me to producing 10 times more & within 3 months, I racked up 4,000 followers from all around the planet.

'Did you ever end up speaking in front of the audience of hundreds of people from your visualizations?'
Yes, multiple times.

Why do I tell you all of this?
It's to get you to think correctly about the law of attraction.

In my case, it really felt like the universe was bending its will to make things become a reality.
1. I visualized it.
2. I allocated my energy towards this direction.
3. I manifested.

That's the blueprint for the law of attraction.

However, understand that for a thought to form into a belief, there should be passion for the action. Even if you don't have passion now, you can later. To develop passion, the mind needs a WHY.

The WHY shouldn't be solely tied to material possession. Otherwise, the mind cannot perceive the bigger picture.

Honest truth?

I started the athletics company solely for the money. I love sports, but I had no passion whatsoever for sports clothing.

My desire was towards speaking & storytelling. It was my hobby that I would do for fun.

What are you trying to manifest?
Are you taking consistent action towards it??
Or are you just visualizing and then taking a nap???

The journey is the car.
Visualization is the destination.
And you are the driver.

It's dope if you know the destination, but without clicking the accelerator, the car is not moving.

So press the accelerator.
Take a few wrong turns.
Learn how to take the right turns after discovering what the wrong turns were.

One day, the destination will be reached.
Then the vision becomes bigger.

Now the mind has another destination.

And another.
And another.
And another.

That's the journey bud.
If you can see it, and the body is capable, then you can achieve it.

Shatter limiting beliefs & use the imagination to paint your destiny.

THE BIGGEST LESSON LEARNED IN 2019

When I graduated with my bachelor's degree in electrical engineering, I was happy. It seemed like all the late nights were worth it.

During my time completing the degree, I was taking a lot of credits. 18, 20, 21 a semester. It wasn't easy. This caused me to spend a lot of late nights in the library. Up until 5 am.

'What kept you going?'
It was the status of getting the degree.

Felt as though it would be 'cool' to tell people I was an electrical engineer. Thought it would have people thinking I was smart.

At age 5, I said I was going to be an electrical engineer. So, I had a genuine passion for it. But the 5 am study sessions? A lot of that was to get praise.

By the time I graduated, I realized something.
'Which was?'
I didn't get the praise that I thought I 'deserved.'

I got a few pats on the back & that was about it. Most people went on with their lives. And I was forced to go on with mine.

That's one of the reasons many musicians have tons of great songs when they are looking for the record deal.

But once they get it?

They fall off. They take their foot off the gas pedal & get lazy.

When they were striving for that record deal, they were hungry. They had ambition. They were fighting for that elusive goal of the record deal. But once they get it, they are a tad bit surprised.

Their life doesn't seem any easier.
It actually seems harder.

There is added pressure of producing a hit for the record labels while getting little praise for it.

The biggest lesson that I learned in 2019 was that you need to be your own hype man & critic.

I heard this advice from many others.
Yet, I didn't understand what it meant until 2019 during some introspection.

Humans are wired to think mainly about their own lives.
Every human has their own problems, worries, desires etc.

When I got my electrical engineering degree, I was happy.
But most of it was drowned out by the resentment that I felt towards others for not being as happy for me.

Just a few pats on the back??

That's all?
Do y'all know how many late nights I went through for
this?!?

I'd like to apologize to my younger self.

It's because I robbed the younger Armani of the joy of
getting something that he put an intention towards.

All because of the opinions of others.

Older Armani finally had his aha moment.

Which is why I had my mom send me a picture of my
electrical engineering degree as 2019 was winding down.

Although it was late, I finally took the time to appreciate
the degree. I gave myself the pat on the back that I thought
I deserved.

That's what we all need to do.

The closest people to you don't really know what happens
behind the scenes. And they spend less than 1% of time
thinking about it.

This may hurt some people.
But it will empower others.
It used to hurt me.
Now I get empowered by it.

It allows me to form a stronger bond with myself
& consciously recall all the stuff that I feel proud of.

Once 2020 began, it was a changed paradigm.
There was a new mantra.
There was a new philosophy.
Future Armani told present Armani:
*'Others will never fully get your struggles, bud. So, you sure as
hell better pick up the slack.'*

When we watch a movie, we only see the 2-2.5 hours of it.
But there were actors, directors, script writers planning
that movie for months (if not years).

We rarely wonder, 'Gee whiz, wonder what all the
logistics behind this film were!'

We just watch the movie, then go about our day.
Other people do the same in context to our lives.

If you are waiting for your pats on the back from others,
then you are going to be waiting for a long time.

Be your own hype man, critic, secretary, and any other
position you can think of.

IS SOCIAL MEDIA WASTING YOUR TIME?

I once saw a tweet which said:
"Social media is a waste of time if you are not building anything."

I did not fully agree with this.
However, I did agree with a good portion of it.
Agreed enough to retweet the tweet.

I don't think you necessarily need to build something to gain value out of social media. But I do believe that building something zones in the focus, which has a lot of spillover effects.

Other than building, another way to get value out of social media is to socialize and/or learn.

The question is:
Are you feeling like you are wasting your time on the vast array of information technology?

There are tons of black and white advice dealing with social media addiction.
-"Drop social media cold turkey!"
-"Delete your apps, go ghost & never even think about using it again!"

This sounds like good advice, at first. Yet, it's not really solving the core issue. Normally, people who try to quit something cold turkey come back to the bad habit. But this time, worse.

Some situations, the cold turkey approach works. Normally when it does work, a lot of shame & embarrassment was involved.

Like a guy who decides to quit alcohol forever after getting a DUI and losing his dream job.

A person will probably quit social media cold turkey if they were involved in an embarrassing position, or a lot of anxiety was formed.

My approach is different. My approach is to first find the value in social media. Find the value in technology.
'Find value? I thought technology was evil?'
Not quite.

The general public often gets certain topics and makes them general. That's how the masses process information. In very binary & sensationalized terms.

Social media breaks down space, time & causation. If that's not a benefit, then I don't know what is.

'You used some words that were a bit technical. Can you break them down?'
I'll sort of break them down.
No need to get detailed.

Let's talk about the daily newsletter that I send to my subscribers. I want you to momentarily envision that you are one of my subscribers.

If you are subbed to the list, then awesome, you don't have
to envision too much. If you aren't subbed, play along.

Now we are communicating in the newsletter.
I am in Tampa.
Where are you?
'Colorado.'
Okay, so space has been demolished.

In terms of time, I am writing this email at 5:59 pm est.
What time are you reading it?
'7:08 pm est.'
Time has been demolished.

Now in terms of causation.
Cause and effect.

Did you read my email from yesterday?
'Yes, the one about dry humor.'
That's correct.

Did you have to read dry humor to understand today's
email?
'No.'
Why not?
'Because the 2 newsletters are not related. The 2 cover
different topics.'
Correct.

The 2 newsletters are standalone items.
Cause and effect have been demolished.

Overall, this was a little example.

You may be like, *well a newsletter is not social media!*
But that's not the point.
Same concepts apply.

The reason I like finding the good parts of social media is that now I can use it more so as a weapon. Rather than being used by it.

To understand how to leverage social media, we need to get a bit deeper.
'How deep?'
We need to know ourselves.

'Come on man. I'm not Socrates or something.'
Well, you're going to have to become a deeper person.
Especially in the world of information technology.

Technology is a mirror image of ourselves. What is possible nowadays would have been considered magic a couple of centuries ago. Scratch that...
Couple of decades ago.

Don't you see?
It's time to wake up.
The advancement of technology on the outside is ironically telling us to wake up on the inside. To gain value out of the world of technology, someone needs to know themselves.

In terms of my life, I don't follow many people on Twitter. Nothing personal.

The main thing I use Twitter for is to practice my writing & thinking skills. That's what I want from the platform.

The sharpened writing & thinking skills allow me to write
long form blogs & consistently put out books.

It's a cascading effect.

I know myself enough to know that the birdy app has data
scientists & engineers trying to keep me on the app for a
long time.

When I follow too many people, I know I may be scrolling
too much. Sacrificing my craft in the process.
The low following count leads to enhanced creativity &
consistency, for me.

But this advice may not work for you.
Heck, it may be detrimental to you.

This is why I say you need to know yourself to make
technology your servant. Rather than the other way around.
Technology & all these social media apps need to be viewed
as a guard dog.

I had this neighbor in my last house who would get bullied
by his dog.
Frail looking guy in his 30s.
Harry Potter glasses.
Would always wear tiny shorts.

I'd see him getting pulled around by his big pit-bull. It was
not an owner walking his dog. It looked like a situation of
the dog walking the owner.

Overall, if you find yourself wasting time on social media,
then understand that's how the algorithms are designed.

It's designed to feed you mental junk food to keep you scrolling.

Awareness is king.

Say the good stuff before you weigh the bad stuff. Once the good stuff has been outlined, it may be an "aha moment" of YOU being the problem.

No offense.

Actually, take offense.
Because by taking that offense, you wake up.
Look into the mirror.

By looking into the mirror, you see a reflection of you.

Likewise, the same computer juggernaut in your pocket right now...It's a reflection of you as well.

Hopefully, it's showing an image that you're proud of.

THE REFINED REBEL

Every now and then, I think...
Which field is without dogma?

When a field scales, it gets saturated.
It seems like innovation takes a halt and people are doing a
lot of theorizing and talking.

One of the finest things is to be a refined rebel.

Refined, to not be a savage.
Rebel, to not be a conformist.

At first, lacking formal training in a subject may seem like
an obstacle. As more time elapses, it may have been a gift.
'Why?'

Because by never (or rarely) being subject to formal
training, it allowed you to explore & experiment. This is
how anyone can be a scientist regarding a certain craft.

Decentralization is a great concept.
However, it always seems like components of centralization
creep up to decentralization.

A couple of years ago, I was taking a course on blockchain.
It was a very technical course.

I learned how the data mining process worked, how the
infrastructure of blockchain was set up & the whole
concept of decentralization.

My professor had been in the Bitcoin game for a long time
and he could talk for hours on it.
Well, he gave me some insights on how much electricity it
took to mine the coins.

A shit ton.

So much electricity, that it's almost impossible to mine a
coin by one's self with a standard laptop. It was smarter to
pair up into groups. Through groups, mining coins would
become much more cost effective.

Well, what started to form were a bunch of big mining
companies. The big mining companies made me think:
*"Wait a minute, I thought this thing was supposed to be
decentralized?"*

I don't know the state of the mining process nowadays. But
I remember that was a class discussion we had a while back.

Same stuff happens on Twitter. On the front end, it looks
like we are so decentralized. We can say whatever we
want! But on the back end, Twitter is a corporation and it
operates like a corporation.

Front end is decentralized.
Back end is centralized.

This is why I believe self-education is a weapon for anyone.
Especially in the world of communication skills.

I never got my master's in communication or anything like
that. However, my path was unique. Which allowed me to
never conform to any ideology.

I have experience as an engineer who dealt with
communications technology. Was involved in Toastmasters.
Served as a communications chair for my BNI chapter in
Tampa. Have a globalized media company in ArmaniTalks.

Was this the standard path? Nope. But this is good.
Because I try to the best of my abilities to remain open
minded. Open minded enough to learn from the world.

Thus far, I haven't gone out of my way to put down any
groups. Because if I do, I may fall for a belief which
eventually gets me to conform.

With ArmaniTalks, there are no middlemen. I don't need
to run my ideas by other people to be like:
'Hey, is it okay if I talk about this?'

The reason that this is good is because it will allow for a
chance of evolution as well. The ideas are supposed to grow
up with me.

The refined rebel doesn't owe anyone, anything.
Actually, scratch that.
They do owe someone, something.

The owe their mind the truth.
That's about it.

Around January 2020, I ran into 2 monks outside of
Dunkin Donuts and decided to talk to them.
How often do you run into monks?

As we were talking, I asked them why their robes were orange. They looked at me and just said:
'Truth.'

When I asked for more clarification, they said that:
'Orange represents fire. Fire represents dispelling ignorance.'

I was stunned.

For **2** reasons:
1. Now I knew why monks wore orange robes.
2. I have a symbol of a fire in my logo.

I never knew why, but the fire in my logo always *felt* right.

It's one of those situations where it seemed like the answer was buried within all along, and it was just a matter of becoming aware of it. Hearing the monk's response to fire representing truth gave me further meaning for my logo.

Overall, the refined rebel has a sense of humility to always adjust and grow. But the rebel side allows them to not fall for herd thinking traps. Allows them to not fall for:
'Well, this is just the way it is.'

When you really know a subject, that's when you realize you don't know anything at all.

The more a subject is learned in detail, the more the language is bypassed. Language is the barrier of entry. But most people stop there.

Language is the formalized structure of OTHER people's concepts. The language is meant to serve as the training wheels, but experiences serve as riding the bike.

When experiences are gained, the mind can form the language from YOUR lens, not someone else's. Through the process of forming the ideas from your lens, that's when the learning process really begins.

Overall, I do see value in formal education. I got my bachelor's & masters. I will never talk down on that.

However, I see plenty of value in self education.
Learning in the streets.
No matter which field you're in.

Be refined so you don't make enemies.
Be a rebel so you don't become soft.

That's balancing 2 worlds to create an experience.
That experience will unlock your inner fire & dispel away all ignorance.

HOW TO CONTROL THE MIND

In order to communicate effectively, you must be able to control the mind.
'And if I don't?'
Then you go on tangents.

You probably had a few times when you began telling a story and ended up talking about a brand-new point without remembering how you got there. It happens. The reason this happens is because the mind is in utter chaos.

Let me give you an analogy to picture the mind. Picture water.

I don't know about you, but for me, water is a win or loss thing. It's either drinkable or not. If the water is brown, it's good as useless to me.

'What does that have to do with the mind?'
Well, if your mind is chaotic, then in many ways, it's good as useless to you.
'Just because its chaotic?'
Yes.

It's like the water that you can't drink.
Think about it.

Most of your acts are done on autopilot. So if your mind isn't giving you direction, then what's the point? Diddly squat, that's what.

Let's say you want to tame the mind. Then the whole
game changes.

The water clarifies.
Now you have clean water. Drinkable.
'How do I get the clean water?'
You direct your mind to something.

There must be something that you are actively working
towards. Not something you hope to do. But
something that you can do in the present day.

As you keep redirecting your mind, it starts becoming
tamed. The mind which was once chaotic is now becoming
obedient.

That's the real cheat code. Direct your mind to something
grand and allow yourself to blossom into something grand.

Try this exercise.
Say: *I will make 10,000,000$.*
Say: *I will provide 10,000,000$ worth of value.*

Which statement made you feel more empowered?
'The second.'
Why?
'It felt like I'm becoming my best self so I can help others
become their best self.'
Exactly. You redirected your mind to your favor.

Redirecting is what eventually allows you to move with
intent & renewed energy. Otherwise, you'll have a whole
lot of wasted movements with nothing to show for it.

When moving with intent, the mind becomes redirected in a structured way. It's generating new thoughts to your favor on autopilot.

What is your grand target?

And whenever your mind wanders off, put it back on that. Bullseye.

ARE THOUGHTS ENERGY?

'Are thoughts energy? What kind of silly question is that??'
Well, is it?
'No.'
Why not?
'Because I can't see it.'
Ah.
So, what do you define as energy?
'Well, I need to be able to see it! For example, I can see a battery working with my eyes.'

So, when you are in a hot room, do you feel the energy of heat?
'Yes.'
But can you see it?
'No.'
But do you still believe it exists?
'Hm... yea.'

All these questions are not meant to get you stuck. Rather, to get you thinking. What is the current quality of your thoughts?

I saw a video almost a decade ago about consciousness & water. When you mutter negative words to water and allow it to crystallize, the crystals look awful. When you recite empowering words to water and allow it to crystallize, the crystals look beautiful.

Thoughts are energy.

When you have negative thoughts about failing, you
FEEL bad. When you have empowering thoughts, you
FEEL bold.

Thoughts are creating an impulse in the body.

Viewing thoughts as energy allows us to be more mindful
about which thought we give attention to. Thoughts can
either cripple you or give you clues.

It comes down to direction.

When you have no direction, your thoughts are very
random. Random thoughts make it difficult to find patterns.
The lack of patterns puts your behavior off into chaos.

When you have a direction, your thoughts can still be very
random. However, now your mission makes it easy to find
patterns. The abundance of patterns puts your behavior on
track.

This comes down to thinking bigger.
You get direction by looking up, not to the side.

All too often, we look to the side.
You look to the side when you compete with others.
When you trying to keep up with the Jones.
You look up when you create a legacy.

No one is your competitor. We all have our own unique
calling & there's enough out there for anyone to win.

Creator > creator & competitor > competitor

Simple.

When you look up, all your thoughts flow in one major
stream trying to help you get to that grand goal.

I heard this great quote once which said, 'we are all born
with our own unique boxes and it's just our duty to dance
perfectly in them.'

What's your box?
Not someone else's.
Once you find that box, you can build on top of that.

Each thought is a brick. Each brick will ultimately help
you create the castle that no one can compete with.

The energy label that you assign to the thought is based off
your life goals. A bad thought or a good thought is
subjective & based on the person.

Jim may view being a celebrity in a good light.
Joe may view being a celebrity in a bad light.

To start seeing the energy behind your thoughts, start
asking yourself, *what is the grand goal that I'm shooting for?*

Are you looking to the side or up?
Are you just a random bundle of thoughts or can
you see patterns?

These are all questions you want to answer so you can
begin tapping into the invisible world of energy.

The world which has all the answers, but not seen by those
who think small.

THE FUTURE OF
TECHNOLOGY

'What do you view as the **3** most important times in
history?'

1. When we learned how to farm.
2. Industrial age.
3. Information age (now).

Each of those moments were a game changer in terms of
history.Without the first **2** moments, we would not get to
right now.

Before learning how to farm, we were hunting. Farming
taught us the ability to think long term & grow
our resources. Learning how to farm changed the game.
Rather than hunting animals all the time, now we were
taming them.

Think about it.

A horse was now being used to move the wagons.
This created the roots for the industrial age.

The big thinkers from the industrial age were like:
'Look, these horses are great. But a machine could do the
job better.'

The industrial age was the birth of the car, railroads, trains,
using oil as a predominant energy source etc.
Now we tamed physical machines.

This created the roots for the information age.

The big thinkers from our generation are now going from physical machines to nonphysical ones.

As an engineer, I witnessed this firsthand.

I still remember when one of my coworkers got fired because his job was being automated. The job which took him 6-8 hours a day to do, was now being automated to a PowerShell script which could do it in 15 seconds.

Crazy to witness.

In many ways, my coworker was the horse that was replaced by the machine. But a nonphysical one.

Don't you see what is occurring? We are being set up to maximize our imagination.

Imagine if we were still hunting all the time?
That is a ridiculous scenario to imagine.

Imagine if we were using horses all the time to get around places. Then we would consider it as 'wasting a lot of time.'

Society is wondering if robots will take all our jobs.
My opinion?
Nah...

The logical jobs will get taken, but the creative jobs will stay.
If your job requires a certain form of imagination, then you're good.

My coworker unfortunately got fired because his job was easy. It wasn't easy to learn. It takes time to learn, study, fail a bunch of times, try again, build proficiency overtime, memorize procedures etc. But for a machine?
Light work.

However, with creative jobs?

They aren't going away.

Entrepreneurs, artists, content creators, realtors, music producers, web designers etc. will stay.

Better yet, creative people are going to use machines to make themselves even more creative. That's where our future is headed.

Let me give you an example. I always considered myself a creative fellow. However, I never knew I could do anything with it. Until the information age happened.

Now I use Twitter to write, YouTube to do videos, website to sell. I'm making the machines work for me.

They will do as I say, but it is my imagination that makes them run.

If a monkey could do your job, then a robot or a script will take it.

A human is a shit computer when it comes to logic.
A computer is a shit human when it comes to creativity.

As the information age grows and become richer, busy work will become automated work. Don't believe me? Google the Internet of Things (IoT). It's closer than we can imagine. I see it becoming more mainstream during 2020-2030.

Bring awareness to the big picture.
What will 20 years from now be like?
Make technology work for you.

Just like our ancestors tamed animals to farm and leveraged machines to produce, we need to think like them.

Technology can take the burden off your hands.
Make it your servant.
Only you rule it.

If you do not take command, then you can bet your ass the machines will *(example: social media addiction)*.

THE BENEFITS OF WRITING EVERYDAY

Writing.
Such a beautiful act.
Writing is one of those skills you want to practice daily.

'Why? I have enough on my plate!'
And writing will alleviate that.

As the information age rises, attention spans will drop.
A reduced attention span will lead to chaotic thinking &
loss of focus.

Chaotic mind leads to chaotic emotions.
Chaotic emotions lead to chaotic behaviors.
Writing daily is more important than ever.

If you are someone who has integrated technology into your
life, then writing is no longer an option, it is a must.
Writing is active meditation.
It grounds you.

Benefits include:
- o   Clear thinking.
- o   Clarified speaking skills (less rambling).
- o   Enhanced focus.

One benefit often not discussed is the *ability to connect dots.*

It is difficult to connect the dots from the past through
reflection alone.
'Why?'

Because many of us can't control our mind.

A person who cannot focus will find it difficult to reflect. When they try reflecting, they will drift off. That's when reflecting turns into dwelling.

Dwelling can lead to getting caught up in past mistakes & 'what if' scenarios from memory lane. That's why people like to distract themselves.

When you can't control the mind, you are scared to be alone with it.

Writing changes up the game.
Writing turns a passive task into an active one.

When you are forced to come to terms with your experiences, that's when you see clearer images than when you viewed them from afar. Seeing clearer images makes it much easier to connect the dots. That's when ideas begin to build upon one another.

Make peace with your past so you can have clarity for the present/future. Habits pick up a life of its own & begin to connect to other habits.

Want to become a creative monster?
Then write every day for 7 months.

Use Twitter for some good. Rather than retweeting pictures of weed & porn, write out 1 valuable tweet a day.

Build an email list for fun, promote it on a social media & write to it consistently.

Start a blog.

If you don't want to do any of that, then a pen & paper
never hurts.

Soon, you will:
-Think of ideas (and very valuables one at that) much
quicker than your peers.
-Begin to see patterns when others see isolated acts.

Writing builds street smarts.
There are few acts like it.

WHY EMBARRASSMENT IS A GOOD THING

I remember a few years ago, I became interested in public speaking. One of the reasons why was because of one of my friends.
Rohan.

He was always a very socially awkward kid.
Awkward body language.
Awkward mannerisms.
Awkward smile.

After years & years of being a very strange fellow, he decided to do something about it. He decided to join Toastmasters.

At first, the rest of our friend group found this to be comical. Public speaking? Rohan is going to talk in front of people?? Too funny.

Let's see what happens.

But despite our mockery, Rohan continued with his journey. At first, we didn't notice any significant changes in him. Thought our prediction about him flopping was accurate.

However, within a few weeks, things began to change.

Rohan began to change.
He became more confident.
His awkwardness melted away.
He had been reborn.

DOES PUBLIC SPEAKING REALLY WORK?

After seeing Rohan's massive life transformation, I realized that he may have been onto something. I decided that public speaking had power.

Which is why I hit up Rohan & told him I wanted to learn the public speaking ways. Well, it just so happened that Rohan & I were in the same fraternity.

Once he found out that I was interested in this new lifestyle, he wanted me to begin speaking up more in chapter.

(Chapter is a weekly meeting that the fraternity members have to keep the organization functioning smoothly.)

I decided he was right.

FIRST PRESENTATION IN CHAPTER

I took Rohan's advice & volunteered to give a 5-minute planned speech. In this speech, I was going to talk about the importance of volunteering for one of our local school events.

Filled with speech anxiety, I prepared like a mad man!

I wrote the speech out, studied it and memorized the whole thing line by line.

'The whole thing?'

The whole thing.

After 4 days of nonstop preparation, the big day arrived. I was called on stage to give this 5-minute talk. That I did.

5 minutes later

'How did it go bro??'

It went amazing!

Got through the whole thing. For me, that was a miracle in itself. But there was a huge problem.

'What was that?'

I had apparently said the word 'uh' around 30 times.

After the speech, a bunch of my fraternity brothers began making fun of me. All harmless humor, but it stung. I had prepared so much & now all I was remembered for was saying 'uh' nonstop.

I was crushed.

WHY IS EMBARRASSMENT A GOOD THING?

After that whole speaking mishap, I felt shame like none other. Luckily, it awakened a whole new side to me. It made me aware of my massive public speaking flaw.

So, I knew exactly what my Achilles heel was. Now, it was just a matter of making moves to take care of business.

For the next few months, I began to take public speaking more seriously. Joined clubs, practiced speaking on my free time, watched speakers etc. I began this new journey out of the blue moon.

After consistent practicing, I had begun to evolve like Rohan had. Building the public speaking muscle allowed me to be taken more seriously. This skill allowed me to move up in my fraternity.

What was initially mocked relentlessly allowed me to one day become the Vice President of my fraternity.

It was the shame that allowed me to spark my journey in the first place.

IS EMBARRASSMENT HOLDING YOU BACK?

One thing that I learned about my whole speaking mishap was that my fraternity brothers found my error to be funny, sure. However, after my failure, they had moved on with their lives.

The only person who continued to think about it was me.

The reason embarrassment is holding you back is because you genuinely think other people will be daydreaming about your failures all day. It's normal to have that worry.

But reality check...
They won't be thinking about you all day.

Let me give you an example.

Have you ever seen someone trip?
'I have.'
Pretty embarrassing for them, right?
'Oh yea, very embarrassing.'
Did you spend all day thinking about it?
'No.'
Why?
'Because I have bigger things to worry about.'
Exactly. Same with other people.

They have daily problems, responsibilities & bills to worry about. You aren't that special to occupy most of their thoughts!

LET SHAME SERVE AS A COMPASS

Use shame as a compass, not a life sentence. Let it serve as a compass for the next big challenge that you are going to tackle. Shame is a fuel that allows you to make massive life changes.

Find out what embarrasses you & make incremental progress to get better. That's fear tackling 101.

Even though my fraternity brothers forgot about my 'uh' mishap, I am extremely happy they pointed out the quirk. I'm happier that they used it as an opportunity to make fun of me.

Without that shame, I would have been blind.
They saved me years of time.

What embarrasses you?
There's tension and perception behind that embarassment.

The only thing preventing you from turning the perception
into a tool is working through the tension.
That tension is simply energy.

Shame is a gift and a curse.
When the dust settles, it serves more as a gift than a curse.

DANGERS OF SOCIAL MEDIA ADDICTION

In the beginning of 2019, I started to see plenty of people post about social media addiction and their encounter with it.

Two posts stuck out:
One was by Victor Pride written a while back & one written by Kyle Trouble.

They both made major points in their articles. The ultimate point?
Social media can affect your mood.

The two of them mentioned how excessive usage of social media had the tendency to either make them feel angry or sad. That was alarming to me.
'Why?'
Because in 2018, I noticed the same...

I focused a lot more on Twitter to get my message out there while I built my website. Having that strong focus on Twitter led me to notice a sense of information overload.

The information overload resulted to a lot of thinking.
The lots of thinking resulted to a disjointed focus.
The disjointed focus led to a poor control of my emotions.

Thought it was a coincidence, until I saw both these authors bring it up.

Which is why I want to warn you.

Social media can absolutely affect your emotions. Our generation is the first guinea pig for social media. There is not 20 years' worth of data to base studies off to get a deeper understanding of its effects on our lives.

Don't wait for the data.
Misguided social media usage will come back to haunt you.

Make yourself aware asap!!
In 2018, my purpose was hazy.

It was a little bit about building a fan base, little bit about learning, little bit about waiting till my site got finished and a bunch of other random stuff.

With a hazy purpose, I had the tendency to stay on social media working in circles. When I did that, Kyle and Victor were 100% right.

With that being said, should you eliminate social media usage?
Nah.

But be smart.
Go in with a purpose.

Are you producing?
Are you learning?
Are you networking?
Are you decompressing & having fun?

Whatever it is, set time limits & don't spend all day just
hanging out there. Take care of business & move on.

Whatever your social media platform of choice is, make sure
you curate your feed & use it as a vehicle for growth.
Do not let it control your emotions.

In 2018, I luckily learned my lesson.

Next time you are on social media for too long, ask
yourself, what's the purpose? Make sure you aren't letting
it hack into your mind & penetrate to your heart.

Stay woke fam.

FROM AN ANGEL TO A SNAKE: STORY ABOUT 2500$

Snakes have cost me time, money & a peace of mind.
Some of the stuff I know now, I wished I knew before.

FLASHBACK

When I was younger, I was naive. Had people lie to my
face many times. But I had this tendency to immediately
forget.

The fact that the snake was being nice to me indicated in
my mind that all was good. The snake must have changed
their ways. But naivety is a normal thing when you are
young. If you find yourself forgiving a lot, do not be too
hard on yourself.

There are plenty of good people on this planet, sure.
However, there are also plenty of evil people on this planet.

SNAKE OR FRIEND?

Who said the two were mutually exclusive?
'Huh??'
You heard me.
Who said the two were mutually exclusive?

Sometimes, I am happy when I know someone is a snake.

It brings me peace.
I know that I would never trust them.

But you know what's scary?
'What?'
You know your great friends?
'Yea.'
There is a chance they can turn into a snake.

'Yea right. You are being paranoid bro.'
I wish I was.
I have a story that I would like to share.

LONER

During my time studying in engineering, I was a loner.
Would spend a lot of time prepping for exams & doing
homework alone. Hated it.

The degree was taking a toll on me.
'How?'
Well, I was barely able to socialize, workout, eat well and
all that.

Test taking was never my thing. And the flux of
engineering exams was not something that I could take
lightly.

This is getting way too hard.
You know what?

There were tons of kids from my class who would study

together.

How about I stop being such a lonely clown?
Time to socialize.

FISHBOWL

All the engineers hung out at a place called the 'Fishbowl.'
'Did it look like a fishbowl?'
Nope.
No clue why they called it that. But I think it had to do
with all the flags from the world hanging on the ceiling.

I decided to check it out after one of my classes.
Many kids from my classes were studying there.
So I decided to join them.
'Was it a good idea?'
Yes!

It was such an excellent idea.

Engineering principles that I would spending HOURS
studying from on Google & Khan Academy were being
explained to me within minutes by smart people. Whoever
thought being social would have its perks?

LONELY NO MORE

After realizing what a cheat code to success studying with a
group was, I ditched my loner ways.

There was a kid who would always be the smartest kid in
the group, no matter which engineering subject it was.

You name it. Engineering systems, differential equations,
wireless communications etc.

For the sake of the story, let's call him Jimmy.

Jimmy was a genius.
IQ was off the charts.
EQ was off the charts.

You know what made everything even cooler?
'What??'
He was Bengali.
Just like me.

I don't think you know, my friend.
But Bengalis form a friendship really quick.
My interaction with Jimmy was no different.

We bonded the second we found out that we were from the
same village.

Jimmy and I were two peas in a pod.
Who would have ever thought?

We were the only 2 Bengalis in our entire engineering
program and got along!
Chemistry was perfect.

TRUE BOND

Jimmy became one of my best friends.
We were like long lost brothers.

After our engineering exams, I would invite him to chill
with my other friend's.

Jimmy was the ONLY kid from my engineering classes
who I invited to chill with the rest of my homies.

The rest of the kids in the engineering program had
dork like tendencies. But Jimmy had this magical presence
that allowed him to get along with everyone.

He wasn't like those annoying kids who would roast you
the whole time when you introduce him to your friend
circle.

He would hype me up. Made me sound like the high IQ
one in engineering. Ha!
He was funny.

BLOSSOMING FURTHER

Jimmy and I stayed friends for a long time.
'How long?'
Until graduation & after graduation.

Here was the thing.
We were both dreaming super big.
We knew that engineering would be our paths for a while,
sure. However, we wanted something bigger.

We wanted to start a business.
'For real? What about engineering?'
What about it? We can do both.
Fuck it.

We will start a business.
To my surprise...
Jimmy already had a game plan ready.

GAME PLAN TIME

Won't go into much detail, but the game plan dealt with
'virtual real estate.'

In summary, virtual real estate was about buying websites.
The main goal was to buy a few websites that were making
a profit & then our goal was to make it more profitable.

What could be so hard about that?
Jimmy and I spent days searching for websites.

We decided to build a dual debit card account so we could
combine our money. This was our business account.

We each put in 2500$.
And to my wonder...

The second we both put in our pennies, a website owner
contacted us back.

WEBSITE TIME

This was an e-commerce site that sold cooking items.
The site apparently made 350$ a month.

'So why did the owner want to sell it?'
Because the site owner wanted to retire to travel the world.

This man wanted to sell us a website that made 350$ a month for 5000$.

Bruh...
This must be a joke.
No way are we getting such an easy deal on our first ever business transaction.

But we were!

I was the guy emailing the site owner about purchasing the website. Tried to negotiate it down a little bit more, but no. 5000$ it was.

The money was sent over to the site owner on Western Union.

And just like that.
We were officially site owners.

SO HOW DID IT FEEL?

Felt like a hassle.

Because now we needed to transfer the files to our hosting services, switch over domain names, and sync their email list to our email accounts etc.

Well, we were SUPPOSED to. But out of nowhere, something strange happened. The site owner messaged me back. He said he needed another 2500$ to finish the full transaction.

Wait, what the hell?
We just paid you 5000$ dollars. What do you mean?

'I need another 2500$ to finish the full transaction,' the
man said.
Huh?

Hold up, let me call Jimmy, something seems strange.
ring ring

'Hello?' responded Jimmy.
*Yo bro, the site owner wants another 2500$ to finish off the
transaction. What do you think? We are so close,* I said.

'Hm.. seems a little strange. Want to cover it? I will get
paid this weekend and I will pay you back.'
Yea, sure.

This was a small hiccup, but no biggie.
I will have 200$ in my bank account after paying the other
2500$. It will all be worth it.

Okay, site owner.
I am about to send you the money now.
No more flaking!

BUT WAIT?

I was one millisecond away from clicking the submit button
on Western Union. Then I started receiving a call.

Who the hell was calling when I am about to make the deal
of a lifetime? Some weird area code. Oh well. Let me pick
up.

Hello?
'Hello, Mr. Chowdhury?'
Yes maam, how can I help you?
'Mr. Chowdhury, did you recently send 5000$
somewhere?'
Yes, why?
'Mr. Chowdhury. You sent your money to an unverified
account in Uganda. You may be getting scammed.'
Huh??

'Yes, do you know a kid named Jimmy Nosun?'
Yes, why?
'The account is registered under his name.'
Wait, what??

'Yes sir. If you know him, I recommend you immediately
contact the police. The money has already been dispersed,
so we are unable to retrieve your money.
What the fuck?

A SNAKE?

ring ring

'Hello?' said Jimmy.
*Hey Jimmy. I just got off the phone with Western Union. They
said the money I am transferring is to an account in Uganda.
They said the name is registered under you. What the heck bro?'*

phone clicks

Did this dude just hang up on me?
I called back.

'The person you are trying to reach is not available, please
leave a voicemail.'

What the hell??
Pick up Jimmy! What's going on??

SILENCE

I called 50 times, at least.
But no luck.

'So did you go to his house?'
I wish.

However, I literally never went to his house. Strange, I
know. But our friendship was formed & strengthened in our
university. He would always say his parents were strict.

'So what did you do?'
I called back another 50 times.
But that piece of shit was not picking up.

Was my boy actually scamming me?
Nah man. Come on. Please don't let that be the case.
Please say he is playing a joke on me.

JOKER?

No.
Not a joker.
This was real.

'Did you call the police?'
No.
'Why?'

I may sound naive if I tell you my response.
'No, go ahead.'
I couldn't bring it upon myself to call the cops on Jimmy.

Something prevented me from calling the police.
I literally had 911 dialed on my phone.
All I had to do was click call.
Yet, I couldn't.

Even though Jimmy did this to me...
All our memories of our friendship were flashing back in my
mind. I still had love for the friend who I thought I knew.

FROM AN ANGEL TO A SNAKE

You read the sub header correctly. Sometimes the story
does not have a rainbows & butterflies ending.

The full transformation had taken place.
The angel mutated into a scaly ass snake.

Still hurts my heart to write this.
A kid who I considered a brother would ruin it all for

money?

I wanted him to be one of my Groomsmen.

Wanted him to be a Godfather to my child.
Talked about how we were going to take over of the
world.

But nah.
Greed got in the way.

LESSON?

What did you learn from this?
Because if it is anything, I want you to pick up one thing.
And I am looking out for you.

Google, your mommy & daddy, the media, the
entertainment industry will not tell you this.

But MOST of the people on this planet are snakes.

SHOCKING STATISTIC

Well, let me clarify that statement. Most people in the
world are snakes in relation to you. That means they only
have their best interests in mind.

Most of the people that you see, they don't give a fuck
about you. They are only your friends because they have
something to gain. Which is why I ALWAYS say keep
your circle small.

The world is **NOT** rainbows and butterflies. The random people who you are telling your dreams to do not have your best interests in mind.

Trust me. They will have o hesitancy to throw you under the bus if need be.

WHAT YOU NEED TO DO

Every single time you give your full trust to someone, make sure their actions back up their words.

NEVER TELL SOMEONE ALL OF YOUR NEXT MOVES.

Maybe your parents or siblings. But never tell an outsider or friend every bit detail. Jimmy was someone who I thought I could trust no matter what.

I was proven wrong.
Always maintain a little mystery.

LEGACY MODE

I want to move in silence.
I want the success to make the noise.

Tick tock my friends.

The Level Up Mind steamrolls those snakes.
No conflict is too big of a conflict.

From an Angel to a Snake, sure.
But that has not stopped me from chasing my dreams.

And snake bites will not stop you from chasing your dreams
either.

We have rhino skin.
Simply cannot be stopped.

HOW TO PERSUADE
WITH CONFIDENCE

With the rise of social media, the term *'influencer'* gets thrown around a lot. Nowadays, it's gotten to a point where anyone with a couple of followers can call themselves an influencer.

But are they really?
Does the follower count dictate persuasion skills?
Not necessarily.

To be honest, you don't even need followers.
You can persuade solely by yourself in the real world.
In the digital world, follower counts help build social authority, sure. But it is not mandatory.

'Then what is??'

Hold on there tiger.
I will tell you.
But first, I need to explain what persuasion is.

My definition of persuasion is:
Altering perceptions to cause a behavior.
Which is why having a big follower count does not mean you are an influencer.

There are many accounts who grew large because they solely provide entertainment. However, do they cause their audience to take any form of action?
Not really.

They provide great entertainment, which is admirable. Still,
is action being taken due to altered perceptions?
That's the key question.

The key to persuasion & influence is doing less.

TAMING YOUR EGO IS MANDATORY. EMPATHY IS MANDATORY.

That's not how you have been taught persuasion. You have
been taught that the person who is the best with words will
cause a behavioral change.
Wrong.

In many cases, that will work, sure.
However, it is not the most effective method.

Which is why taming the ego & empathy are mandatory.
These 2 moves allow you to enter the other person's world.

Every human has a perception map.
A perception map is their reality.

Their reality is made up of their unique life experiences,
relationships, friendships & all of that. The perception map
of a human is like a fingerprint. No one has the same exact
ones.

This is why the goal of persuasion is to enter the other
person's world. Find out the language they use, the way
they think, their opinions etc.

'Well, what if I don't agree with their viewpoints?"

That doesn't matter. Understanding does not equate to
agreeing.

Push past the ego & understand away.

Next, you must be clear about what you want them to do.
What is the action you want them to take?

If you are reading this right now, then somehow you were
influenced to buy this book.
The action taken was to purchase.

There needs to be a precise intent.
Without it, you will be having an aimless conversation
about nothing.

Finally, ask strategic questions to get them to your intent
or provide so much value that they make the decision
for themselves.

Path 1: Strategic questions that direct them to your intent

These questions will allow them to think that they thought
of the idea themselves. No one likes to be sold to, but
everyone likes to be sold.

Counterintuitive, I know.
But human nature is tricky.

Path 2: Immense value

You provide so much relevant information that speaks
directly to that person's world that they want to know
what's next!

In that case, you drop a call to action in the bottom.
At this point, they will feel silly for not acting after all the value you gave them.

Both ways work.

This is why a person with 1,000 followers can have more influence than a person with 1,000,000 followers.

The 1,000 followers' guy may know exactly what their market wants, addresses those pain points & helps give an action plan that will take them away from the pain.

While the guy with the 1,000,000 followers is posting cat videos & piling up likes.

WHAT J COLE & KEVIN HART TAUGHT ME ABOUT LIFE

In the fall of 2009, a few of my classmates came to me and asked me if I wanted to go to a concert.
What kind of concert? I wondered.

My classmates looked at me crazy & one of them asked: 'Bro, it's our college's homecoming. And you are asking what concert???'

I asked them who was going to be performing.

One of them said, 'This up-and-coming artist named J Cole.'
Who?? I wondered.
But eh, I'm not doing anything, I'll go.

By the time we went, the concert was empty.
There were tons of open seats.

I wonder who this J Cole guy was & why he couldn't even fill up a college campus. But it didn't matter that the concert was empty, J Cole still killed it.

Fast forward a few months later, and now it was Kevin Hart who was going to be doing a comedy routine. We knew him as the guy from 'Soul Plane' & 'Scary Movie 3,' nothing more.

Kevin wasn't even the main act! He was opening for a comedian by the name of Bruce-Bruce.

Even though Kevin Hart was not the main act, he gave a great performance. The whole audience was cracking up & we were baffled that he wasn't more well known.

Why did I bring up these two individuals?

Because after fast forwarding 10 years, their lives are completely different.

Millions of dollars, tons of lives impacted & in the top echelon of their professions.

What I respected about J Cole and Kevin Hart was their come up. When they were not as popular, they still had this level of passion you could sense. A part of me thinks even without the money, they'd be doing what they were doing.

The beauty about digital media is that we can now see people's rise in real time.

Unfortunately, there wasn't Snapchat & Instagram back when I saw them performing. Otherwise, I could have held onto those videos + photos and bragged to my friend's about how I saw them before their rise.

I recall Jamie Foxx once telling a story on a late-night show about throwing a party a few decades ago. The people in his party who came were ordinary back then.

Nowadays, they are Jay Z, Kanye West, Jennifer Lopez etc.

You never know where someone can be in 10 years.
You never know where you can be in 10 years.

Often, we focus on day-by-day levels. But significant moves happen in the present day when the mind is conditioned to think fast forward.

Not the type of thinking fast forward which leads to anxiety & stress.
More so the type of thinking where a person is grateful for the present moment & tactically considering the future.

For the time being, keep an eye out for people who seem very gifted. Keep an out for yourself when you do something special.

Who knows where anyone will be in the next few decades...

SOCIAL ENERGY

I was once watching this debate between a bunch of scientists, spiritualists, and generalists. The goal of the debate was to understand the fundamental nature of reality.

Everyone seemed chill. It seemed like they were all open minded & ready to learn each other's viewpoint.

However, there was this one smug scientist. Forgot his name. He acted like a *know it all.*

He was saying why he was right & was talking to everyone else like children who didn't know any better. Most of the people he was lecturing were much older than him & more experienced in their given field.

This smug scientist had such a poor attitude.
It was enough to throw off the entire harmony of the interaction.

That was a great look into the world of social dynamics.

Social dynamics does not work like the linear world.
In the world of logic, from 10 apples, if 1 apple is bad, then only 1 apple is bad.

In the world of social dynamics, from 10 humans, if 1 human is bad, then it has the capability of having a more profound impact. Why?

It's because humans by themselves are complex systems.

A complex system is when a bunch of random parts create a
unified whole.

Group those complex systems (humans) with other
complex systems (humans) and now you just made
that complex system much more complex.

In the world of systems, there are **2** fundamental energy
types:
Synergy
Or
Dysergy

Synergy is when the multiple moving parts work in
harmony & amplify one another. Dysergy is the exact
opposite.

The more I learn about complex systems, the more I
appreciate great leadership. A great leader needs to manage
a bunch of egos (individual parts) and guide them towards a
unified goal (grand mission).

In debates like this, it is up to the moderator to take on the
role of a leader. When the moderator does not do his job,
then **1** bad apple is all it takes to impact the complex
system.

Social energy is a profound concept in social skills. That's
why the older someone gets, the smaller their friend circle
gets.

Sometimes, it's by choice & sometimes, life just happens.

It's good that the dwindling friend circle happens because
the friend circle also serves as a complex system.
Unfortunately, some people become toxic as the years go
by.
They become that mean, close minded scientist who thinks
they know it all.

That's a mistake.
We don't know it all.
The second we think we do, that's when social energy
begins to no longer favor us. See if you can spot the social
energy in different interactions.

From content, to debates to offline communication.

Social energy is a part of humans like their eye lids.
Become fluent in that energy through observation &
through the act of feeling your feelings.

HEARING OUT BORING PEOPLE

There was one year I was serving as the External Vice President of my Toastmasters club. Which was the position for the member who got the name of Toastmasters out there.

The goal was to get others to hear about the club & bring more people into our meetings. It was a great position.

Being in that position, I had to work alongside the president a lot. Mainly so we could be in communication with the updates. The president's name was Brenda.

Brenda was an amazing listener.
Top tier at that.

My club had a position called the Quizmaster.
The Quizmaster would be responsible for hearing all the speakers for the meeting and creating unique questions based on each speech.

Then the Quizmaster would ask the questions at the end of the meeting to see if the crowd was paying attention.

Brenda would always have the answers. Her arm would spring up when the Quizmaster would ask a question. I liked that about Brenda. She was an amazing listener.

'I feel like you're about to set up a big BUT.'
I am.

BUT the only thing I did not like about Brenda was how she was boring & long winded.

She had this tendency to speak for a long time.
Yes, she was an extremely polished speaker.
Never would mess up her grammar.

But she would always need to get every single word out there. No summaries in her book.

This became an issue because what I thought would be a quick 5-minute update call would always turn into a 45-minute call.

Fam, I got stuff to do.
Get to the point.

It was tough listening to her.
So much mental bandwidth was needed.
To make matters worse, this was someone I would have *multiple* meetings with throughout the week.

What was I to do?
That was a tough lesson about listening through the pain.

One common answer would have been to let her know that she was long winded. However, something in my gut said that it was not the right thing to do. No matter how polite I made it seem.

Something in my gut said, just aim to listen.
Listening through the pain is a mighty soft skill.

This was what I learned.
There are a lot of Brenda's.
Plus, there are people much worse than the Brenda's of the
world.

Brenda's talks always had a point.
Even though she took an awfully long time to explain it.

Many never have a point.
They just talk to talk.

'Why is listening through the pain a good thing?'
Listening through the pain is a good thing, second.
It's a needed thing, first.

The reason why is due to the complexity of any system.
We can't expect a life where everyone gets to the point
quick and fast. Where listening is effortless.

In a complex system, it's always smart to expect poor
speakers.

This is a similar analogy to driving.
Doesn't matter what kind of driver you are.
At one point or another, it's smart to expect traffic jams.

Listening through the pain becomes even tougher when you
know exactly what this person is trying to say, 50 words
early. When you know the subject matter.

And you're doing, 'mhm, mhm, mhm.'
Trying to imply, 'I got it!'

But they continue speaking on.

That's when the ego wants to jump in and finish the
sentence.

Sometimes, that's needed.
Other times, this is a great opportunity to listen through
the pain.

There are 2 lives.

1 life is when we listen just to be polite.
The 2nd life is when we listen so we can sharpen our own
mind.

In the latter life, listening becomes a selfish & selfless
process.

I've heard concentration levels determine greatness levels.
Well, listening is concentration in the social world.

And proper listening is much more than just nodding your
head like a bobble head doll.

BENJAMIN FRANKLIN &

CHRIS BROWN

When I was in the 11th or 12th grade, I was getting ready to go to prom. My date was this girl named Katherine. I didn't want to take Katherine. She was this stalker girl I had in high school & was mad annoying.

'Then why'd you take her?'
Because I had no clue that I wanted to go to prom.

Thought most of my friends wouldn't go.
Last minute, all of them changed their minds.

Katherine was one of the last girls who wasn't asked. During the limo ride to the prom venue, Katherine kept talking about Chris Brown.

This was around the time Chris Brown was charged with physical abuse on Rihanna. It was something that all the girls in the limo kept talking about.

Chris Brown was branded as the next Michael Jackson during that time. Was his career over even before it began?

However, we didn't talk about that too long.
Once prom started, Chris Brown was an afterthought.

As over a decade has passed by since that moment, I marvel at how Chris was able to turn his career around. Nowadays, he is a hit maker, just like he was back then.

But you can tell from his personality, there are good & bad sides.

Something about a person's eyes.

You can tell if they have a lot of stuff that haunts them.

I feel like all artists have some level of that haunted feeling. Channeled darkness is what inspires a lot of their art in the first place.

The man Chris Brown has issues to this day.
Who doesn't?
It's a part of being human.

When looking closer, it's easy to tell that Chris Brown is gifted at what he does.

A blend of a rapper, singer, dancer & I think he paints too.
That's a lot of creativity.

It's easy to view the phrase 'genius' in terms of academic standards. Yet, that's not the full definition of a genius.

A genius is someone with supreme intellectual OR creative abilities.

If you were to ask me, Chris Brown is a creative genius. He is only in his 30s, so his skills will just mature more from here on out as long as he doesn't do something reckless.

'But what does Chris Brown have to do with Benjamin Franklin?'

Good question.

Benjamin Franklin was a multi-talented individual.
He was a businessman, inventor, politician & scientist.

It would have been normal if he was just average in all of
those different fields. However, that was not remotely the
case.

He is one of the nation's founding fathers. On the political
sphere, that's top notch. But as a scientist, his work with
electricity?? That's top notch as well!

Some can say his experiments that led to the harnessing of
electricity is just as captivating as the internet. Without
electricity, the digital world does not exist.

'So, Chris Brown & Benjamin Franklin were both gifted.
But why are you telling me this?'
I tell you this so you can think bigger.

The unique thing about learning is the cross combination of
subjects. How you cross combine subjects is how you leave
your unique imprint on this planet.

It's not enough to just learn public speaking anymore.
Instead, you want to web public speaking, with the ability
to write, tell jokes etc.

Get it?
This is a cross combination of subjects.

I have a friend who is excellent with Microsoft Excel.
Rather than just using Microsoft Excel at work... He

combined the tool with his eCommerce business to create synergy. He runs simulations, creates forecasting & a whole bunch of other useful metrics by cross combining 2 fields.

Chris Brown and Benjamin Franklin were both geniuses in their own ways. Maybe you weren't the most gifted academic wise. In the real world, academics is just a small part of the game.

It is creativity that allows a student to cross combine subjects to become an animal that will never be duplicated.

Creativity is the hottest commodity as the internet age continues to mature.

Don't niche down too much.
Create your own niche.

DO YOU OVER WORK?

I've always been one of those guys who felt guilty for
resting. When I would rest, I felt like I was slacking off.

A few years ago, I had a roommate who was the exact
opposite. He would not only rest but would have a great
time doing it.

This man was obsessed with sports & fantasy football. He
would work his 9-5 job and come back to watch any game
that was on. If there weren't any games on, he'd watch
Netflix.

My workstation was set up in the living room, so I would
be in the vicinity of his chill sessions.

At times, I would be insanely working on my masters,
business, or my job. Every now and then, I'd peak my head
up to see what was going on with him.

There he was, ass plopped on the couch, eating Doritos &
watching TV away.
At peace...

A part of me wanted that peace.
But whenever I tried to rest, I felt tense.

A part of me felt sorry for myself when I rested too much.
It had gotten to a point where I was forgetting how to
rest.

So, on a busy day, I decided I was going to push the work back for the next day and I joined my roommate on his TV watching session. He was watching Sons of Anarchy and was happy to have company.

As we were watching the show, a part of me was automatically drifting off to the work I had to do. How I was 'falling behind.'

The rest session ended up feeling like hell.

As time went on by, I started noticing I wasn't the only person with a problem like this. I met many others who found it difficult to rest.

From famous athletes, musicians & other friends. They just over worked.

Forgetting how to rest is a problem. A problem that goes unnoticed because it seems like productivity. But it is not productivity. Over working takes away peace.

Once we learn the foundations of a skillset, we transition from working with our body to working more with our mind. Like when we drive, even though it is physically with our body, it feels like a mental act now.

Well, when the mind isn't sharp, that's when you make silly mistakes.

Have you ever had that moment where you worked strong for months on end to only have your body shut down...and then you became a lazy sack of shit for months on end?

'Ya bro, that's happened a lot!'
That's because your body wants rest. When you refuse to give it that, it will take rest for you. This is why you need to learn how to rest.

If you're someone who doesn't consider yourself an over worker or overly ambitious, then these ideas won't really click with you.

But for over workers, the first thing to start off doing is to learn to schedule in the rest session.
When you rest, just rest.

The scheduling is key.
The reason I felt all worked up watching Sons of Anarchy with my roommate was because I didn't plan ahead of time for it.

You don't want to plan too much to a point where you are over working on something new. It should just be a general gist.

I used to relax mainly at night.
After all my work was done.

A hack I learned is to find a hobby that allows you to relax & then build a life around that!
So you are relaxing all the time.

An example in context to my life is the storytelling done with the ArmaniTalks brand.

I like writing & speaking, so it's a way for me to relax.

Nowadays, I use the ArmaniTalks brand as a vehicle for me to always have fun.

In context to your life, things may be different.
Can you find a hobby that allows you to chill?

The best hobbies are the ones that can make you creative, healthier and/or money.
Find a hobby like that.

Overworking should be acknowledged.
It's not pretty & takes away your serenity.

Some of us may have no option. We probably are trying to get something off the ground & it's requiring a lot of time and energy. If that's the case, find a way to incorporate relaxation into it.

Working is like patience.

If you're being patient with a sour attitude, then you're just waiting, not being patient.
Patience is a mindset. Waiting is physical.

Working with a sour attitude jades you over time. It makes you eventually quit. Sprinkle rest in there so you move with enthusiasm.

Enthusiasm beats hard work because enthusiasm makes it easier to do hard work, which eventually turns into smart work.

HOW TO BE PROUD OF SOMETHING

Being proud of your accomplishments is a great thing.
It allows you to acknowledge how far you have come.
What are you proud of?

A few years back, there were **2** things that stuck out. One was my black belt in Tae-Kwon-Do. Another was my master's degree in systems engineering.

-The first accomplishment stuck out because it worked out the body.
-The second accomplishment stuck out because it worked out the mind.

But there's something I noticed.
'What?'
I had to physically see it to truly feel proud.

Once **I SAW & FELT** the black belt, it was a different feeling.
Once **I SAW & FELT** my degree, it was a different feeling.
I will talk about why I capitalized these 2 words shortly.

Nowadays, what makes me proud is my email list & website.
It's because I own it & it's **2** things that I am building from ground up.

But do you notice something?

'No, not really.'
Well, you should.

A big reason for not feeling grateful for stuff is because it is
kept within the mind.

The mind is a wonderful entity.
It's capable of using logic, creativity, imagination and much
more. But the mind can be a place where things get lost.

This is why people who are super ambitious often seem the
least fulfilled. It's because they undermine their past 8 wins
& are off to the next one. You'll be surprised how many
wins we are completely blind to because we lack a basic
gratitude practice.

The reason I capitalized the words, SAW & FELT,
earlier was because I got my senses involved in terms of my
win.
It made everything real.

That's not to say you need to touch & feel up on
everything to feel like a winner.
Trust me, you shouldn't do that...
You may get in a lot of trouble.

But what this brings awareness to is the technology of using
your 5 senses to the best of your ability.

-Take those progress pictures as you are picking up that
new diet.
-Upload those blog posts as you launch that website.
-Record those videos as you are traveling to that new
country.

Things can often get lost in your mind due to the fast-paced nature
of life.

I have a folder in my laptop & a section in my home for
things that I'm proud of. From my degrees, first white
labeled product, Toastmasters ribbons etc.
This is the confidence zone.

You have had wins in your life.
At this point, probably too many to count.
So slow down.

Take them from the mind to reality.
Create a space for those wins.
Whether it's digital or analog.
Doesn't matter.

The key is to embrace that the wins were YOURS.
Not someone else's.
That's something no one can ever take away from you.

THE MEAN AUDIENCE MEMBER

I used to be in a class called Engineering for Professionals.
It was a class to teach engineers about soft skills.

A few of the basics:
How to network, dress up, write persuasively etc.

One of the other acts we had to do was public speaking.

The odd part was that we didn't learn any public speaking.
Our professor, Mr. Breckenridge said:
'Pick a topic & get ready to give an 8-minute presentation
on it.'

8 minutes seems like light work.
However, for a person who hates public speaking? It feels
like an eternity.

The next week, each of us were going up one at a time
presenting our topics. It was a wide range of material.

Some people talked about their love for cooking.
Others talked about a sport they played growing up.
Some people talked about their first internship.

Everything seemed to be going well.
It seemed like everyone was going to be laid back.
But that was not the case.

There was this bitch named Adam.

He had a long beard, 5'4 ish height, skinny & a snarky
smile.

'Why did you call him a bitch?'
Because he made it the intent to make each speaker look
like a fool.

You see, we had a question-and-answer section after our
speech was done. This guy would keep asking "Gotcha"
questions to make the speaker stumble.

For one of the speakers who was talking about their love
for cooking, Adam was like:
'You *claim* to be a chef. But you working alongside your
dad growing up makes you a Sous Chef. Do you even
know what that is?'

Then the crowd would await to hear the speaker's response.

Seeing Adam blatantly be so disrespectful put a lot of
anxiety on the other speakers. They were wondering what
sort of condescending question Adam was going to ask
them.

This caused the entire vibe of the classroom to be thrown
off. I could hear Adam giggling and doing this ridiculous
smirk anytime someone would stumble.

The day I went up, I was talking about my most recent
internship in an aerospace company. Talked about my time
working there & the project that I worked on.

After I was done, Adam's hand sprang up.

Then he proceeded to ask these questions raising doubt that
I worked on the project at all:
'You *claim* to have worked on this project. But you never
went into detail about the hardware & software of the
equipment that you *claimed* to have worked on.'

It's an 8-minute speech bud.
I didn't know I was supposed to tell you every single last
detail.

Adam wasn't asking the question to become more well
informed. He was asking the question to make me stumble.

After class was done, I was angry at this dude.
Face was super-hot & I felt like everyone was staring at
me (they weren't).

Once the class bell had rang, I went to confront Adam.
Nothing violent. But just to see why he behaved the way
he did.

This clown had a rollie backpack & would walk with his
eyes staring at the floor.

Hey man, why were you trying to embarrass me like that? I
asked.
'Huh? What do you mean?' asked Adam.
*You were asking these questions with a condescending tone. Not
only to me, but to everyone. What's your problem?* I asked in
anger.

That's when he looks at me all confused.
'My bad bro, I have no clue what you are talking about.'

The way he was responding now versus in class was night and day.

He seemed like a calm, composed kid, now.
It's like he was trying to put on this tough guy persona when he was in class. Other than that, he was super soft spoken.

You may be wondering what the lesson of this story is. To be honest, it is vague. Just like human nature is supposed to be.

To this day, I have no clue why Adam acted like that when asking others questions or what he was trying to prove.

Then again, we often have no clue why people act the way they do. We think we know once the act has been committed. However, that's why the hindsight bias exists.

This story goes to show that the ball is always on the speaker's court. To go with the intention of being the most prepared that you can be.

The Adam's are highly rare.
Plus, the Adam's do not win the other audience members over. The other audience member's find people like Adam to be repulsive.

From the grand scheme of things, the audience wants you to do well on stage. They rarely actively want to see you fail.

I don't know if Adam even wanted me to fail. Or if he was just a quiet kid who felt heard when he was asking the 'tough questions.'

Just know that the public speaking world presents different challenges. Challenges that they do not teach you in books.

The beauty is that public speaking is a crash course on becoming anti fragile.

Not only are you okay when conflict hits.
You get better when conflict hits.

No matter how bad it gets, it ultimately comes down to how you perceive the information.

As a few years have gone on by, I thank Adam.
You gave me a great lesson, my friend.

With you, I became tougher.
Now I have an extra data point to refer to in the future.

Embrace the Adam's of your journey.
They will only make you stronger.
That's when the battle tested speaker will rise within.

HOW TO FIND YOUR TRIBE

Back in the days, I was the type of guy who would filter my personality to make sure that I was liked by everyone. I would just agree a lot & act like a people pleaser.

Did I make friends? I guess.
'What do you mean, you guess?'
Well, I had quantity on my side. But for some reason, those people didn't feel like my friends.

They were just a bunch of people that I had surface level bonds with. They had no clue who I was. I was simply wearing a mask for approval, and all that bought me was despair.

A few years later, I switched up my strategy & thought, what was the point of having friends if I treated it like a job?

So, I took of the mask and was reborn as my authentic self. The nice guy had been replaced with the guy who would occasionally curse, crack jokes & aim to have fun.

Results?

A lot of people were rubbed the wrong way & distanced themselves from me. But there were also a handful of people who remained. The ones who remained became my tribe members.

Since altering my strategy, my circle has reduced, but my happiness has skyrocketed.

I now have strong social bonds with my smaller circle.

At that point, I discovered:
You can only consider someone a friend once they have seen your authentic side on multiple occasions.

Understand that:
-It is abnormal for everyone to like you in the social world.
-It is normal for everyone to not like you in the social world.

When this concept is truly registered, the attraction process is sparked. You are not chasing people anymore. No, no. You are magnetizing the right people and repelling the wrong people. Win-win if you ask me.

A cheat code to attracting people into your tribe is to talk to a person like you've known them for your entire life. This is harder than it looks. Luckily, it can be practiced. Especially when it's set as the intention.

Not sure if you are aware of it or not, but each interaction leads us to talk to the person like we have known them for our entire lives. It's a game of just setting that as the intention in the beginning of the interaction, so we aren't talking in circles.

This is when the most authentic side comes out.
This whole nice label is a pretty lie.

Niceness will destroy your life.

Niceness will have you reflecting with regret.

Authenticity is what stands the test of time.
Unless authenticity is set as the reward, the second place of niceness will be the fate.

PUBLIC SPEAKING MINDSET

What do you think is the most important factor of public speaking?
'How well you speak, of course!'
Nope, try again.
'How well you move on stage?'
Nope, try again.
'You serious? Umm.. how well you make the audience feel involved?'
Nope.

'Damn! Now you're just messing with me Armani.'
I'm not.
'Then what's the most important?'
Mindset.

'Mindset?? Come on now, that's the last of my worries.'
No, my friend, that is the most of your worries.

It is your mindset that dictates your life.
In the public speaking arena, it is no different.
Your mindset will make or break you.

'I'll be honest bro, I have no clue how my mindset should operate.'
No worries, I got you then.

I have 5 years' worth of Toastmasters experience, have spoken in conferences, keynote speeches & spoke to

hundreds of people at weddings for a few best man
speeches.
'Did you learn anything?'
Yes, plenty.

Believe it or not, after giving over dozens & dozens of
speeches, I noticed something breathtaking.
'What was that?'
Patterns.
'Patterns?'
Yes.

The beauty about patterns is that those are the core
concepts! The core concepts are what is really needed to
master any skillset.

'So public speaking can be learned?'
Yes.
Read on...

WHY THE SPEECH ANXIETY THO??

Before I explain these core concepts, I want you to
understand why you have speech anxiety in the first place.
Making sense of the anxiety makes you feel in much more
control, melts nerve, disarms judgment & allows you to
adopt new beliefs much more easily.

The reason that you have speech anxiety is because you
were rarely taught public speaking growing up.

Think about it, how many classes throughout your life were
you given on public speaking?
'Umm.. I took it as an elective in college.'

See? That's barely anything!

Many of you didn't even take that elective. I know I didn't.
That's like me giving you a car for the first time ever &
saying, *go figure it out.* How would you feel?
'Terrified.'
Exactly.

So the main reason that you have speech anxiety is because
you are underinformed. Let's change your mindset now.

CORE CONCEPT #1: NO, THEY CAN'T TELL

Most of my Toastmasters mentees weren't scared of the
speaking part. They were more scared about looking
nervous in front of the crowd. They thought if they were
feeling nervous, then they will look nervous. Looking ugly
in the process.

'Well, was it true?'
Nope.

People can NOT tell that you are nervous from your appearance.

Take some time to research the 'illusion of transparency'
after reading this. It's when you think your internal nerves
are leaking out to the external public. Obviously, be aware
of your body language. Fidgeting & squirmy behavior is a
different story.

Now, for the quivering voice.

This voice is typically a problem in the first 20-30 seconds of a speech, max. But it goes away on its own. Most quit too soon to understand that it melts away. The audience mainly remembers how you finish.

This core concept should now allow you to feel more comfortable on stage.

Once you internalize this concept, you will feel much more comfortable in your skin.

CORE CONCEPT # 2 YOU ARE THE STAR

I am not joking when I say this, but you are the big deal. Too many people come and ask me, 'what can I do to make the crowd like me??'

I'm like, *who cares if they like you or not?*
The question is, *do YOU like them?*

All the people in the audience have regular days, worries and bills to pay. You are their gateway into a new world. They will go on the journey that you take them on with your speech.

This mentality shift melts away the needy behavior & helps you feel much more confident & in control. Trust me, the audience will love you more for it. They can literally feel your energy.

Which leads me to core concept #3....

CORE CONCEPT #3 NOT WHAT YOU SAY, BUT HOW YOU SAY

Your speech needs to have a clear purpose & theme. But the exact words don't necessarily matter to the audience.

This is good news for you because now you don't have to worry every time you say a filler word, stutter, or have a grammar mishap (don't overdo it of course).

'What are they placing most of their focus on?'
Your energy. Write this down:
Public speaking isn't delivery with your sentences, it's delivering with your energy.

Get it?
Just show enthusiasm about your topic & you'll immediately connect to their primal side. That's what they want. A speech with a purpose that is delivered with enthusiasm is your recipe for success.

CORE CONCEPT #4 ABUNDANCE MENTALITY

You bring speech anxiety upon yourself when you view public speaking with a scarcity mindset. It's very daunting to give a speech when you think that this speech will be your ONLY chance to prove yourself.

Ditch that limited way of thinking.
Think big. There is no shortage of speech opportunities in your lifetime.

Remember, every time you get on stage, it's a win.
Always.

You being brave already puts you in front of the wimps
who watch from the sidelines. Never forget that. You are
winning every time you step foot into the battlefield.

CORE CONCEPT # 5 YOU CAN ALWAYS LEVEL UP

Public speaking is no different than any other skill.
You just keep getting better & better with time.
The journey is the greatest part.

I remember when I gave a speech in front of 500 people, I
was like, *I gave a speech in front of that many people and I feel
unfulfilled. Why?*

Because I had a poor mindset back then.
I viewed it like I was done with my journey. Thought of
public speaking like a final product. However, it's not. You
can always get better.

As I keep on gaining more speaking experience, I want to
share my insights with the world to help them as well. I'm
going from learning mode -> learning some more mode &
teaching mode.

Always be in level up mode when you overcome your
speech anxiety. Your speech anxiety will melt away if you
show heart.

The question is, will you keep showing heart after you conquered speech anxiety? That's a question that you can only answer.

MIND OVER MATTER

Those are my 5 core principles.

How many times did you see me talk about the fundamentals of building a speech, eye contact, word choice in any of my tips?
'None.'
Exactly.

That's because these 5 tips will give you the power that you've been wanting all along. The power to speak in front of others.

Once the mind is right, then the small level tasks will be a piece of cake.

THE TIME 1 GOT BACKSTABBED ON TWITTER

One thing I love about Twitter is how it brings different
people with different skillsets together. A great experience.

One day, one of my Twitter followers hopped in my DMs.
He turned my pinned tweet into some dope animation.
It looked great.

He said he was an up-and-coming creative entrepreneur &
said he wanted to show me what he was capable of.
I was impressed.

I personally didn't need the animation service but asked
him what else he could do. He listed off a bunch of skills...
and eventually said 'podcast editing.'

I was going to be launching a podcast, so thought he would
be a great fit for editing my audio.

Let's call him John.
John gave me a price that I thought was reasonable & we
struck a deal.

The next week, there was this semi-big account that
started beef with me. Kept tagging my account & talking
shit. He was an anonymous account who wanted to agitate
me into blocking him. He thought I'd bite.

But nah. I don't block accounts, yet. I just used this semi-big account as entertainment & laughed at how I was living rent free in his head.

As this account was talking shit, I noticed something.
'What?'
John was contributing as well. He was retweeting the tweets bashing me and laughing at the jokes.

The semi-big account clowning me? All good.
I got thick skin.

John clowning me?
Now it's an issue.

Here I am, about to do business with this bum.
Even said I would give him a shoutout if he did well.

I had 11,000 followers at the time & he was scratching 35.
A shoutout would have given him some clout.

But no.
John was a snake.

The next day, he hops in my DMs and enthusiastically asks when he can expect the first podcast episode.
Little did he know, I saw everything.

I'm assuming he thought I blocked the semi-big account. Which is why he felt so bold in expressing his discontent towards me. That seems like the only explanation. No one can be that stupid.

I told him the business deal was off. No way was I going to
work with some guy who seems to lack principles and social
intelligence. I cut him out & never talked to him again.

'Don't you think you're being a little mean?'
No, not really.

I think a snake deserves less.
After that point, I couldn't care if he made a penny from
Twitter or not. You don't bite people who try to help you
out.

However, the bigger lesson was that this whole internet
thing is a derivative, not the source. Which means that the
internet is not reality. But will come off as it.

John can be a completely different person on the internet
than in real life if he wanted to and I see that.

The orange is the source.
The orange juice is the derivative.

Real life is the source.
The internet is the derivative.

Despite the orange juice being a derivative of an orange, it
sure does have a similar taste. I know the difference
between orange juice and apple juice for that reason.

The derivative does not fall too far from the tree.

John's betrayal made me angry because his girl had just
dumped him 2 weeks before and he asked me for tips on

getting out of the rut. Gave him a lot of my time to help
him back up. Didn't ask for anything in return.

That's the thing with social skills.
It's all about knowing that it isn't always pretty out there.

I'm an optimistic guy.
But I'm not stupid.

My optimism doesn't blind me to the darkness of human
nature.
A lot of these people are vile, disgusting creatures with a
harmless face. I see through that.

The older I get, the less I trust.
Thought it would always be the opposite.
I'm an optimist with myself & lean pessimist towards
others. I try to not expect anything from anyone and am
pleasantly surprised if they contribute favors and value.

The internet is a platform where you may be fooled into
trusting someone quicker.

'Wow, what a nice default picture this person has!'
scrolls through 10 tweets
'Wow! I resonate with all these tweets.'
subconsciously trusts them more
'Wow, he is so nice in the DMs!'
may talk a little too much

I'm not telling you not to trust anyone on the internet.
Just beware of trusting too soon.

Nowadays, I get a good chuckle out of the story with John.

John's story is memorable.
Betrayal is the beginning of a lot of memorable stories.

WHY PARETO PRINCIPLE IS KING

Pareto principle states that roughly 80% of the effects come from 20% of the causes. I first heard about this principle when I was doing banner & popup campaigns for affiliate marketing.

I paid this guy named Sebastian a couple hundred dollars to mentor me into getting my first successful campaign.

I created 10 campaigns. He said only 2ish were going to be profitable after repetitive testing. He said it was due to the Pareto principle. I was 22 at the time & never heard of the phrase. But hey, he's the mentor.

As time elapsed, he ended up being right. Awesome! The Pareto principle has just been noted. I thought this law was just applicable for affiliate marketing. Didn't think it was applicable to anything else.

A few years later, I ended up being in the leadership team for Toastmasters. There were 10 of us.

What was mind blowing was that 2 people mainly did most of the work. The others did work too. But it was nothing major that was driving growth for the club.

2 people predominantly pushed the needle.

Okay...
Maybe these are just coincidences.

Recently, I was looking at the analytics for the ArmaniTalks website. That's when my mind was blow again.

There were 2ish articles that were pulling in most of the traffic for my site. Other articles were putting in work too. However, 2 of them were clearly the top dogs when it came down to making significant moves for the site.

After seeing the Pareto principle take life in 3 different contexts in relation to my life, I was sold. This concept was not only for affiliate marketing. It was a life law.

Do you have a Pareto principle moment in your life? If not, then just wait up.

I never noticed the Pareto principle from the get-go. It always took time.

The time gathered data.
Then the data allowed a select few to rise.

Around 2015, something similar was going on in the NBA. The Cleveland Cavaliers & the Golden State Warriors kept meeting each other in the finals. They went to meet each other for 4 years in a row.

It got to a point where a lot of people were like:
'I'm not even watching the regular season! We all know it's going to be the Warriors and Cavaliers going head-to-head.'

Those were the 2 head honchos.
No one messed with them.

Currently, you may have those few acts that move the needle forward. Even if you don't know what they are, just wait up.

222

When you notice the Pareto principle in multiple facets of your life, that's when your mind will be blown. It's the select few that push you forward. Work hard first, so you can enter the territory of working smart.

WHY ACTION MAKES YOU SMARTER

One of the biggest complaints about Toastmasters is what I like the most about it.
'What's that?'
How they never really teach you public speaking.

When first joining the club, I thought I was going to sit in a lecture hall where I was going to learn how to build a speech. Nope.

I was thrown straight into the fire.

Sure, there were resources to help me understand the mechanisms of a speech. But during the club meeting? It was all about doing.

This was a phenomenal strategy because it short circuited the over thinking process and sparked action.

If there was a big lecture and tests to determine whether I understood public speaking or not...Then there would have been a sense of false pride.

I got an A on the test & now I think I can give a speech!
Incorrect.

The beauty about doing is that you can always learn the theory after. When you have personalized experiences to attach the theory to, that's when learning becomes fun.

The way we traditionally learn is the exact opposite way.
Formal education teaches the theory first & at times, gives
some action.
Still, that action (real world experience) is not always
guaranteed. If you trace back into any major innovation, the
reverse has always held true.

People didn't first dissect the science of fire & then create
fire. Instead, fire happened, and they did their best to
engineer it later.

The reason action leads to making you smarter is because it
installs the right habits and helps you ask questions to
problems you never knew you were supposed to have.

For my 3rd speech in Toastmasters, I noticed I was out of
breath 3 minutes in.
'Why?'
Because my collar was too tight.

Wear a shirt that fits, not rocket science.
But until I encountered that problem, I had no clue that I
was going to expect that problem.

I doubt any theory would specifically talk about that
problem in a way where it resonated with me. It required
me to face the problem on stage in front of a live audience
to acknowledge this lesson.

When data has been accumulated, you get the most out of
information.
This mindset alone will cure a lot of procrastination.

Procrastination is when we over consume the theory which
has us constantly consuming more.

Pull the trigger fast.
The theory is not going anywhere.
But your time is.

15 minutes of doing + 50 minutes of learning theory > 15
minutes of doing > 50 minutes of learning theory.

Works like this for any field.
Become smarter by taking action.
Lead with the heart first & back it up with the intellect
second.

Hurt and Never Healed

A lot of years can go wasted because you took the advice of someone who was hurt & never healed.
I see this a lot on social media.

A person can say whatever (lacking any form of logic) and repeat it many times. Then, there will be a segment of the population parroting that ridiculous statement away.

It's insightful.
Yet, sad at the same time.

-Why do hurt people give advice?
-How can we spot hurt people giving advice?

Hurt people require a vehicle.
It's a mode of expression.
Content is a permissionless media to express.

How can we spot hurt people giving advice?
They speak in generals with a somber tone.

The human brain is only capable of taking in so much data. I heard the numbers regarding it recently and it was staggering.

There are trillions of bits of data all around us.
However, at any given moment, the human is only capable of absorbing 2,000,000 bits of that data.

From the 2,000,000 bits, only 150,000 of those bits are processed.
'What determines how the bits are processed?'
We process the bits based off the story in our mind.

This is why 2 people can look at the same exact things but interpret 2 completely different things.

This is why storytelling has always been important.

Mankind only gets a little peak of the world around them, mistaking it as reality. Experiences can easily be fooled.

The body & senses are not always reliable. I know you know what I'm talking about if you ever watched a very scary movie.

cough *Texas Chainsaw Massacre & Paranormal Activity* *cough*

I know that it's a movie.
I know that it's not technically real.
However, my narrative mind is temporarily being fooled.

Heartbeat racing.
Palms sweating.
Dry mouth.

If a movie can fool us, don't you think life can pull a fast one every now and then?
Think about it.

Well, with the limited bits of data that a person is processing, they are basing it off a story in their mind. This causes generalizations to be formed.

Generalizations are the default part of the mind.
Nuances are earned.

That's not to say that speaking in generalizations is always bad.

If you asked me to talk about dolphins, I would be general on that topic vs the person who is a marine biologist. They will know the different types of dolphins and data on it.

The mistake is in thinking that the general is the full story.

Sometimes, the general gives a solid baseline of data.
However, other times, it can lead to awful judgement.

Hurt people speak in extreme black & whites.
It will satisfy some. However, for individuals who seek the nuances, something will always feel missing.

I see this on social media a lot.
I have an account on Facebook which I rarely use but check every now and then.

There are different personality types.
One group is always generalizing:

-Everyone in this gender acts like this.
-This political party only has racists.
-This profession is all full of scammers.

This is why I say developing emotional intelligence is more important than your IQ score. Lack of emotional control leads to impulsive statements.

Trying to use the intellect to mitigate an emotional tsunami is a difficult task. This is why logic is highly important. But what's key is self-awareness.

-Intelligent people are not always self-aware but self-aware people are always intelligent.

'Isn't it sad that so many people fall for the advice of someone who was hurt and never healed?'
Eh.

'What do you mean eh?? Have you no empathy?'
I do. But I believe this is a lesson that needs to be learned the hard way.

Taking advice too quick from poor people can lead to a lot of regret. Hopefully the regret charges up the person to build their own experiences & flex their reflection skills.

Therefore, it's a necessary evil.

No matter which field someone is in, they are given a flurry of suggestions. However, in the information age, anyone can say anything. I could say the sky is red every day for the rest of the year to my Twitter following.

Then 10 of the people from my 30,000 followers will begin thinking, 'this dude may be onto something.'

Then those 10 would want to convince their friends that
they sky is red. They want to be the first to break the
news. A lot of people love being the first to break the news.
It leads to pleasurable emotions.

Remember, other people are going by their story. Every
now and then, there is a person's story who we resonate
with.

The resonation should not mean that we listen to
everything they say. We can have 10 things in common, but
the 11th thing can be completely opposite.

The mind isn't a bicycle.
The training wheels need to come off.

Learning the art of thinking is earned.
Never given.

OSHO

Osho was a famous/controversial spiritual figure in the 70s
and 80s. There is a documentary about him on Netflix.

A couple of weeks back, I saw a channel on YouTube
called OshoTalks. The title of the channel resonated with
me since I have ArmaniTalks.

I listened to his videos & noticed how different he was than
a lot of spiritual people I've seen.

He talked about how he loved luxury.
He wasn't fond of being poor.
Osho talked about the beauty of having wealth.
It was art to him.

Then, there was a line where he talked about the heart vs
the mind. How one took power over the other while it was
supposed to be the other way around.

The mind controls the heart for most people.
Heck, that's how I lived life for many years.

When the mind controls the heart, gaining creativity at will
seems difficult. Mainly because we become more linear with
the thinking.

He continued talking about how the mind is supposed to be
a faithful servant to the heart.
Only then will there be synergy created.

-Working only with the mind, eh.

-Working only with the heart, eh.
-Leading with the mind, and backing it up with the heart, eh.
-Leading with the heart, and backing it up with the mind, that
was what Osho was talking about.

How is all this practical?

As I have been growing up, I realized we know a lot of words but we don't know the true meaning of a lot of those words.
One of the words is wisdom. Wisdom is the portal towards entering the heart in a systematic fashion.

Wisdom formula for me is:
Knowledge + How the knowledge ties in with experiences.

To get started, the knowledge needs to be quality knowledge. Just because Cosmopolitan said it does not mean that it will satisfy the wisdom formula.

'Well, where am I supposed to get knowledge like that?' That depends on each one of us.

Information theory gains knowledge through inference, perception and/or a trustworthy source. That gets difficult. Who is this trustworthy source?

At times, it may be someone we personally know who has lived a well experienced life. Other times, we can refer to ancient texts. Whether it's the Quran, Bible, Bhagavad Gita etc.

You don't have to agree with each word of the texts.

If it's an ancient text, the goal is to understand the lessons
and be able to read through the symbols.

Overall, it's a game of trying to understand knowledge that
may be outside of you.

'Why can't I strictly use my experiences? Why do I need
to learn from others in the first place?'
This part is important.

Because we never fully have all the information.

An immature person thinks they know it all.
A mature person knows that there can be that ONE
experience which SUDDENLY shifts their idea of what
life is.

You ever had that moment?
When you were hardcore on one side.
Time passed by...
Now you were hardcore on the other side??

Which one of you was correct?
Wrong question.

It's better to not even answer that question.
I just asked those series of questions to prove that we can
never fully have all the answers. So, it's good to always be
in learning mode.

Next, this knowledge needs to be able to extract
meaningful data from our experiences. This is when logic &
mind control is key.

I've heard:
'I was just living my truth.'
'Well, I feel, I feel, I feel....'
'My heart told me to do so.'

These all sound good. However, connecting evergreen
knowledge with experiences require a blend of humility,
precise logic & an open mind.

Journaling can help. Depending on the level of mental
control, meditation can help.

Why am I saying this?
It's because that's the formula for wisdom.

Once we unlock wisdom, it's when we are capable of living
in the heart, then use the mind when needed.

Different people say this in different ways.
Some call it, living in the present.

Eckhart Tolle talks about the Power of Now.
It's the same thing that Osho was saying.
When you lead with the heart, that's when you are in a
present state.

However, this needs to be a *systematic* process.
Otherwise, vain impulsiveness will be confused as intuition.

Vain impulsiveness benefits no one other than yourself.
While intuition on the other hand...
Has the chance to benefit many others.

When the heart leads and the mind follows, that's when a prolific attitude can be unlocked.

Surprisingly, this state is not as foreign as we may think. Picture a pretty shocking moment that occurred to you out of nowhere and you could do nothing but accept it.

Maybe it was a betrayal of some sort, someone stole from you, got beat up etc. The body heated up & the movements became slower.

The intellect was turned down. You may have suddenly felt fearless once the anger subsided.

Because if that very bad moment occurred, what else can you exactly fear? Think of a moment like that. At that moment, you were living in the exact present moment.

The heating of the body is a sign of living in the present.

Osho had an interesting philosophy of life.
I like his living in the heart insight.

My only addition is that logic should never be abandoned. The human mind is an especially important tool once we learn how to use it.

-When we live in the heart too much and ditch logic, we may go to no man's land.
-When we build wisdom, that's when we can live in the heart & strategically use logic like an art form.

That's a beautiful synergy.

WHY ARGUMENTS HAPPEN

Have you ever seen one of those posts breaking down how to become a millionaire?

Find a product at this much cost.
Get this much margin.
Sell X amount a day.
Get money.

Then the post does a reverse engineering of the math to wrap it up.
'That means you just need to get 8 sales a day. Now go become a millionaire!'

Normally, a post like this goes viral.
It's very popular.

-With a viral post comes love.
-With a viral post comes hate.

A lot of people are seething with anger looking at this post.
-Only if it was that easy!
-What about taxes?
-What about inventory costs??
Etc.

That's when **2** different worlds begin arguing.

One group is like:

"Chill homie. This post was mainly about giving a big picture understanding."

While another group is like:
"The original poster was intentionally being sinister!"

I can understand both groups very well because I have been in both groups myself. I have been a big picture guy in my life and I have been a little picture guy as well.

If you have fallen into both spectrums as well, then you may know exactly why the argument is occurring.

It's because the 2 groups are speaking different languages.

My personal philosophy is mixing the 2.
Big picture thinking is artistic.
Small detail oriented is engineering.
Artistic Engineering.

It's the best mental model in my opinion because it can answer so many questions in life. Seeing the nodes and seeing the links.

The problem is that formal education often focuses on just the details. Little picture thinking. All the classes are divided into their own unique clean boxes. That's why so many people got outraged by this post.

On the other hand, the reason that the post did go viral was because many people understood the intent.

This post was not meant to appeal to the details.
It was meant to appeal to the heart.

'Ah, the heart. Come on man, now we are getting blurry.'
The language of the heart is a language.

Same concept happens with music.
There is a group of people who love lyricism.
Then there is a group who just wants to vibe.

I had **2** friends a couple of years back.
DP & James.

Those **2** one day start smoking & were like, *'yo Armani, you mind playing some music?'*

I eagerly pull up Eminem on my phone & connect it to the speakers. I started playing 'Cleaning out my Closet.'
Then I turn the volume all the way up.

The **2** look at me like I'm the one smoking.
Looking at me like I'm crazy.

'Bro, turn off that trash! We tryna vibe.'

I was shocked that they would call Eminem trash. So I asked them what they meant.

They said that Eminem wasn't trash. But this wasn't the right moment for them to listen to Eminem.

If you're not familiar with Eminem's music, he is very graphic, lyrical & aggressive. If you are just trying to chill, then that's probably the last thing you want to hear.

Point being, different moments require different languages.

In my opinion, it's a game of priming the mind to see the invisible links while seeing the nodes. One world is not favored for another.

However, one world may serve more useful than another depending on the context.

As I wrote this, I had big picture thinking.
As I edit this, I have little picture viewing.

Both serve a role. Arguments occur when one side tries to convince the other side why their side is better.

Both are ignorant.

Half artist.
Half engineer.

This is one of the cases where 1/2 + 1/2 leads to an answer far greater than 1.

CORRECT WAY TO POLARIZE

Polarization gets a bad reputation in the social dynamic's
world. When people hear polarization, they think:
'Oh my, it seems like I am ruffling some feathers!'

In a way, you are.
But that is a good thing!
It is impossible to be loved by everyone.

Want to know something even deeper?
It's impossible to be hated by everyone as well.
It just doesn't happen.

Picture some of the most despised people around the planet.
If you look closer, then you will see they have die
hard supporters as well. Even serial killers have their own
fan clubs around the world.

Weird as fuck.
Human nature does not make much sense at all, I know.

You can't be fully loved or fully hated.
So, what next?
There are two paths.

- o Path **1**: If I am fake, I will have people who love
  me & hate me.
- o Path **2**: If I am real, I will have people who love
  me & hate me.

Which path sounds more pleasant?

I already know you are choosing path 2. But what's ironic
is that most people spend life adopting path 1.

How do I know? Because I used to take path 1.

I thought if I was a synthetic version of myself, then
everyone and their moms would love me. However, that
was not the case. I still had haters & friends.

So, I altered my approach.
I decided to transform from *synthetic -> authentic.*

In return, I still had haters & friends. But this time? I
was way happier with myself. I realized I was going to get
the same outcome either way, so why not at least go out
being real?

That's how to correctly polarize.

Be yourself & magnetize the right crowd, while at the same
time, repel the wrong crowd. The goal is to get people who
like you, to love you & people who hate you, to do
whatever they want.

Don't spend time trying to convince people who are iffy or
have a distaste towards you to like you.
Not worth the energy.

Let them do their own thing. Just focus on *your* tribe. That
tribe eventually becomes a marketing team. They will stand
for your brand even when you leave the room.

It's strange how simple all of this sounds.
Yet, there is a part of an individual that wants acceptance.

Even if it means ostracizing the same group who welcomes
them with open arms.

You are not lonely, my friend. But that is being perceived
temporarily.
'Why?'
*Loneliness happens when we overlook the people who support us
& dwell on the people who don't support us.*

The ego always looks for satisfaction.
The heart is already fulfilled.

Your tribe is waiting for you to open your arms.
Living on planet earth leads to polarization.
Chasing greatness leads to even more polarization.

Who said polarizing was a bad thing?
It only becomes bad when staring in the wrong direction.
Turn around...

THE SOCIAL SUPERPOWER

In a world where hard work is derided & being lazy is rewarded, people have opted to take the easy way out in many facets of life. They look for shortcuts, loopholes, or the magic pill.

Picture this.

Tom has been struggling to make money on Amazon for months. But then he starts seeing his buddy Mikey make money on Shopify. Tom's eyes light up when he sees the Shopify screenshots.

So instead of continuing forward with Amazon, Tom jumps ship because he believes the new path will be easier.

But no...

Shopify has its own level of variables that take time to figure out. Since Tom has taken the shortcut, he abandoned all the progress he made on Amazon & now has to start over.

Progress = Delayed.
This is a perfect example of when taking the shortcut has made the journey more difficult.

However, it doesn't always have to be like that. A shortcut can help you when you have already built some acumen.

With experience, it's easier to know what to avoid and
what to zone in on.

Well, that is what I am going to be providing you.
It is the social shortcut of a smile.

The smile is a highly underrated social weapon.

Look around you. So many people are so angry all the time.
Well, I do not know if they are angry. But they sure as
hell look like it.

When someone looks angry, they become unapproachable.
They lock out social opportunities even before there was an
opportunity to get it started!

Or let's say you are having a conversation, and the other
person is displaying uncomfortable body language. You are
saying all the right things, so you have no clue what is
wrong.

I have a clue.

It's because you look like you are about to kill them at any
moment. The resting bitch face is absolutely a problem.
Whoever told you it wasn't was lying.

People are visual creatures & it's time we leverage this
knowledge.

Go in front of the mirror & smile.
Do you look creepy?
If so, then you will come off as creepy to the other person.
Adjust.

Squint your eyes more.
Make the smile warmer.
Prioritize comfort.

Do you look more approachable now?
If you saw yourself standing in the street, would you want
to say whatsup?

Or at least ask yourself for directions??
If so, then you're on the right track.

If you look approachable, then it will be much easier to
start & maintain a conversation.

-A smile releases endorphins in someone else's brain.
-A smile releases endorphins in your brain.

Endorphins are feel good chemicals. This is a win-win
situation for both parties.

It's little tweaks like this that builds confidence. It only
takes a few tweaks like this to create a brand-new
personality.

A personality that magnetizes people & radiates warmth.

WHY YOU COMPARE YOURSELF TO OTHERS

I once had a friend ask me why he was always comparing himself to others. Even though he had a lot of things to be proud of, he always felt a little empty.

This friend had a great job, a great family & was making a solid amount of money. Why the emptiness?

After talking for a while, we went from his present day to his past.

This gentleman grew up in the Eastern culture where traditions are a lot different. He grew up in China & immigrated to the U.S at a young age.

As we talked more, I was able to see exactly what the issue was. His parents moved from China to the U.S so my friend could get an education.

When he came to the U.S, it was obvious that his parents were always setting high expectations for him.

-The grade letter B was seen as a D.
-The grade letter C was seen as a F.
-Everything below that was seen as uncharted territory.

Every time he stumbled & got a B or lower, his parents were quick to bring up how the other kids were scoring.

'You know Jackie got an A in the same class you are struggling with. What do you have to say about that?' his parents asked.

After a while, the message became loud & clear.

His parents constantly comparing him to others during his childhood had manifested into its own beast in his present-day life.

I am not saying that his parents were bad people by any means. If you look closer, it doesn't really matter which culture you're from, East or West. Pretty sure you were the victim of being compared to others by an authority figure at one point or another.

If it was before the age of 7, then it was something that stuck for a long time.

In the era of social media, the highlight reel life & technology, we find ourselves comparing our lives to others on the daily.

Even if we get a major W, we are not grateful for it. Instead, we are thinking about how the other person got 2 W's. This is an incredibly sad way to live.

'What advice did you give to your friend who was always compared to others growing up?'
I told him that the past was the past.

Now it's his duty to work on engineering the future. There's no point in moping around & wondering about 'what if' scenarios. May sound harsh, but it is true.

This friend could not turn back time & tell his parents to stop comparing him to others. But he could work on his present-day life & prevent himself from comparing his kids to others.

One of the best ways to recondition your mind towards thinking about how far you have come vs. how much you have left to go is by leveraging gratitude.

Every morning, force yourself to write or say stuff that you are grateful for. Could be a small win or a massive win, doesn't matter. The key is to do it daily, so a rhythm is built.

Begin the morning with it so you can set the tone for the day.
End the night with it so you can set the tone for the next day.

Soon, you will see yourself reversing years of subconscious programming. No more looking at what others are doing & bitching about it.

Take it a level further.
Adopt Level Up Mentality.

A mentality that has you no longer competing with others. Rather, you are now getting inspired by them. You choose what you like about your peers & implement it into your everyday life.

Then go on a **LIFELONG** competition with your prior day self. Your prior day self is an enemy & must be defeated at all costs.
 So, defeat that prior day self at all costs!

MAKING ANXIETY WORK FOR YOU

Anxiety is a feeling of uneasiness about something in the near future. There are **2** forms of anxiety:

1. Event-based: This is a certain event that has you worried.

2. Ambiguous: This is when you are anxious but have no clue about what.

Both feelings are crippling for sure & have you in a state of unease. Let me ask you a question:

For the last major event that you were anxious about, were you more anxious during the buildup or the actual event?

'Hm....'

I don't know about you, but it's typically the <u>build-up</u> that's tougher than the actual event. The perfect example is public speaking.

I used to be terrified leading up to a speech. So terrified that I would plan out every single scenario that would go wrong & how I would be the laughingstock of my community forever.

But while I was giving the speech?
Some nerves in the beginning, sure.

However, not bad at all while the speech progressed. I'm pretty sure I just described a similar theme with many of your anxious events. You feel more anxious during the buildup than the actual event.

ROOT OF ANXIETY

Anxiety happens when you spend more time in your head than in the present moment. Anytime you are feeling anxious, you are thinking way too much.

'Yea, I am always overthinking nonstop.'
So you need to fix it.
'How?'
By staying in the present.

'Any idea why I spend so much time in my head?'
It is due to us living in the information age.

People are swarmed with nonstop information daily. Social media, TV, Netflix, blogs, podcasts etc. You are being flooded with more information than your brain can process. All this consuming has your brain thinking nonstop. Your nonstop thinking is becoming a default behavior.
   o   Nonstop thinking = Anxiety.

Let me hit you with a few formulas that worked for me. I am no anxiety expert, so if you have any serious medical conditions, then go to a doctor. These are just a few ways I turned my anxiety from crippling feelings to a weapon that I leverage.

MY FORMULAS:

I discovered one of the best ways to conquer anxiety is by going from your head to your body.

We don't want this to be a one & done thing.
We want this to be a permanent lifestyle.

In order for you to go from your head to the present, you
need to be able to incorporate a few things into your life.

1. Creativity:
Remember earlier how I mentioned that you were
consuming way too much information since being in the
information age?
'Yes.'

Well, that is way too much energy that you are absorbing.
Unprocessed energy turns into anxiety. Which is why you
must release this energy back into the world.

My recommendation is by producing some form of art.
This is step 1 to making anxiety work for you. All that
energy that you feel within will be released in your latest
story, painting, cooking a new dish etc. Get creative!

2. Mindfulness:

Incorporate mindfulness into your life. Mindfulness is pretty
much consciously checking yourself whenever you are lost
in your thoughts, so you can come back to the present.

Keep repeating the checking in process until it becomes a
lifestyle.

3. Anxiety Reframe:
Anxiety = Negative perception + Intense feelings
Excitement = Positive perception + Intense feelings

Consciously focus on changing the perception towards anxiety. We want you to switch the perception variable, so you view anxiety as excitement.

To do this, ditch the burying method that you most likely have been doing. Burying method is when you act like your anxiety isn't there. Very short-term thinking with o long-term results.

Instead, do the replacement technique. Acknowledge the feeling of anxiety & replace it with a positive thought.

Anxiety is when you worry about everything that can go wrong. So, play fire with fire & replace that thought with everything that could go right.

This part will take a lot of consistency to make moves. But each time you do it, consider it a rep for your mind.

Just like one rep in the gym won't get you muscular, one mental rep won't melt anxiety.

4. The others:

I mentioned the 3 above because they are stuff that you are not always seeing in search engines as effective anxiety busters.

However, the traditional anxiety busters:
-Gym
-Meditation
-Journaling
-Breathing exercises
-Playing sports

-Sleeping right
-Eating right

These all work too. Incorporate as many of them into your life.

Start of small but work your way up from there.

CLOSING THOUGHTS

Anxiety is a man-made term. Our ancestors had no clue what the fuck anxiety was. They just FELT the energy.

From here on out, anxiety is simply energy that will propel you to the next level.

Many people will not pick up the challenge because it requires work. Which is why many people will be used by their anxiety.
But you?

Nope.
Be different.
Make anxiety work for YOU.

THE HIDDEN BENEFIT OF YOGA

A few years ago, I started the p90x program. For those of you not familiar with it, it's a workout program. 90 days of an athletic regimen to not only look good, but also feel good.

One of the workouts was yoga.

Most of the workouts were intense. A lot of burpees, 1 legged tricks, pull-up variations etc. I thought yoga would be light work.

But it wasn't.

Yoga required a good amount of effort. Once I was done with it, I'd feel like a million bucks. Something about yoga connected me to all of my body. Prior to yoga, I didn't see a relationship with my right bicep & left quadricep.

After my sessions, I saw a connection.

Learning is the process of neural pathways intertwining. That's why the person who is always learning is getting more creative day by day. Their neural pathways are connecting in new forms, leading to an emergent property of creativity.

Similar effect with the body.

After I practiced physical yoga, the nerve fibers began
intertwining in new ways. I felt whole! The emergent
property was confidence.

That was the hidden secret of yoga.
A stronger bond with myself.

There are tons of yoga's out there. The one that is the most
familiar to the mainstream is called Hatha Yoga. This is the
one where the body is leveraged in different postures.

However, there are tons of different yoga's out there.

One of the best resources to learn a practical application of
Yoga is the Bhagavad Gita.

The book covers 4 particular paths:
-Bhakti yoga - yoga of devotion.
-Karma yoga - yoga of selfless action.
-Jnana yoga - yoga of knowledge.
-Raja yoga - yoga of concentration.

Hatha yoga isn't covered in that particular book. But that's
what YouTube is for.

Feeling whole is one of the main elements of confidence
and communication.

During high pressure moments, the body is going to be
firing off all sorts of signals. The disjointed mind feels
pressure. The whole mind feels alive.
Yoga is a practical practice that can bring a level of calm in
a busy world. It's much more than stretching. It's a way of
life.

LONELINESS

'Why is loneliness on the rise?'
It comes down to connection.

The quantity of people you know doesn't matter.
It all comes down to connection.

If you have a laptop & look for **WIFI**, chances are that
you'll pick up a lot of signals.

But what if you don't know the password for any of them?
'Then I won't be able to connect.'
Exactly.

All the **WIFI** signals will not do it for you if you don't
have the passwords. There will be no connection to the
internet.

The same concept holds true in social dynamics. All the
people won't do it for you if you don't hear each other out.
There will be no connection. That's when loneliness
manifests.

Social media has made it easier to be surrounded by **WIFI**
signals without passwords. Nowadays, you can have friend
lists of 3,000 people on Facebook. But only 5 are people
who you are genuinely cool with.

Loneliness is an internal journey.

People who are always surrounded by the most people are
the loneliest or fear being alone. That's a losing strategy.

Everything from the external world comes and goes.
The purest stainless steel will rust. A hurricane can knock
over a tree which has been around for ages. The more you
seek happiness from the external world, the lonelier you
feel.

The internal world is the main constant.

Working out teaches this life concept. Ramon set the goal
to rep a heavy weight 10 times. But by rep 6, Ramon
starts FEELING PAIN.

Shh....
Ramon, go to the breath & continue.
Rep 7... *The pain rises.*
Rep 8... *The pain is unbearable. No way will there be a 9.*
Rep 9.... *Whoa, Ramon sees he is getting close. Ramon focuses on
the breath again.*
Rep 10.

Eventually, all the intense pain melts away.
The muscle tensions came and went.
Ramon's breath stayed by his side.
That was the constant.

Most of these people you try to impress won't be around in
a few years. They are going to be doing their own thing.
Moved away. Focused on their own problems.

When you are lonely, it means you are supposed to be
lonely.
'Huh?'
Keep being lonely until you get to know yourself.

'How will I know when the job has been finished?'
When you realize you were never lonely.
Simply alone.

HOW TO JUDGE LESS

You ever had that moment when you were almost done
with something...But last second, something happened that
messed up your groove?

A few examples:

- You're having a good dream. You're about to get to
  the sweet point. Then out of nowhere, the alarm
  clock goes off.
- You are building a house of cards. You're on the last
  part of the house to put on the final touches. Then
  out of nowhere, someone sneezes & it comes
  collapsing down.

Those moments.
The worst.

Recently, I had one of those moments with the lawn
mowing guys in my neighborhood.

There have been a handful of times when I am on the last
20 seconds of a YouTube video. Then out of nowhere, the
lawn mowers in my neighborhood go off. The loud noise
from the mowers drowns out my audio & ruins the entire
video.

'Why don't you just edit those parts out?'
Because I don't like editing out anything in these videos.
It's to exercise concentration.

So, when these fuckers mess me up in the last few seconds, I have to start all the way over.

After it happened a few times, I tried to figure out when they normally came to cut the grass in the neighborhood.

After a few weeks in, I noticed it was on Mondays & Wednesdays around 12-4 pm. Alright cool. I'll record the videos earlier then.

During one Friday, I am about to wrap up an 18-minute video without any screwups. Then in the *last 20 seconds*, I hear the lawn mower go off.

What??? It's Friday!

Not Monday or Wednesday. I played by your rules!! And you guys still screwed me over like this? Let's just say I judged those folks hard. Didn't like these guys messing up my schedule like this.

'That sucks. You must still hate them to this day, right?' Well, not quite.

There was one week when I started to go for a walk after my gym sessions. The gym I go to was 25 minutes away from my apartment. So I went to the neighborhood right next to the gym to walk.

On my path, I noticed there were a few abandoned houses with HUGEEE grass. So big that it didn't seem safe to walk around there. It seemed like there may have been snakes hiding in the grass. So, I took a long path around those houses.

One day, during taking my alternate route, I wondered:
'*How come no one cuts these people's grass? Don't they know how much of an inconvenience they are being to all the other people in the neighborhood?*'

At that moment...
Like a lightning strike, I had an epiphany!

That moment made me appreciate my lawn mowing guys so much more. Made me feel really bad for judging them. What made me feel worse was undermining the work they were doing.

In my neighborhood, the grass is always polished & on point. Never seen it get like the neighborhood with the abandoned houses. That's because of the service these people provide.

That day, I learned the dangers of judging too soon.

The thing with judging is that it happens fast. So fast that it often happens in a subconscious manner.

People judge for different reasons.
- *They may judge from incorrect narratives.*
- *From past experiences.*
- *From present annoyances.*

For me and the lawn mowing people, it was a mix of all 3.

What melts judging is more information or knowledge. Sort of like when I got more information regarding the abandoned houses.

Introspection helps too. But at times, we are unaware when we are judging because it is happening so quick. Therefore, we may not know what to introspect about in the beginning.

It's about learning 'how to judge less' not 'how to never judge again.'

I think there are people who never judge at all. But I'm not one of them. I aim to judge less.

-To be curious, assume someone is smarter than they are.
-To be patient, assume someone is dumber than they are.

A bridge between the **2** is where judging melts.

Getting in between that bridge is hard because it requires conscious focus + tamed ego.

Those lawn mowing folks taught me the art of seeking more information. The information wasn't gained the next day. It took a few months.

Information does not always present itself. It requires seeking from the person who is looking to judge less.

Getting the wakeup call to judge less too soon normally happens through pain.
'When does it happen?
When we, ourselves, were unfairly judged too soon.

THE WORST PUBLIC SPEAKING ADVICE

Cartoon shows can teach kids life lessons masked as entertainment. These lessons can skyrocket the child's learning curve. While some of the other lessons can be misleading.

One advice I would see in different cartoon programs was: *If you're nervous during a speech, then picture the audience in their underwear.*

When I was in the 5th grade, I didn't have too many vehicles to get information. It was either the library or Google. Google didn't have much of the in-depth content that it does today.

Mid way into the 5th grade, my school had the annual spelling bee competition coming up. The winners from each class would be called to compete in front of the school.

All the students from my class lined up & we began the classroom spelling bee.
25 people started.
1 person remained.
That 1 person was me.

I was the winner in my class & now had to represent.
I was no longer doing it for myself.
Instead, I was doing it for Ms. Jacobson's class.

I wished I didn't win.

'Why?'

Because competing in front of my class was light work.
I was talking in front of the same students I was always
surrounded by.

But for the competition? There were going to be hundreds
of people in attendance.
I was nervous.

How was I going to speak in front of all those people?
I asked my friend Arsenio for some advice.

He confidently responded:
*'Bro, you just gotta picture the audience in their underwear.
That'll calm you down.'*

Hm...
I did hear this advice before, so why not?

The day of the spelling bee arrived, and the gym
was packed. I was uneasy.

One by one, each of us went up.
Finally, it was my turn.

Soon as I got called on stage, I was told to spell 'awkward.'
Nothing too bad.
Any dummy could spell that.

As I was trying to spell it, I was also trying to picture the
audience in their underwear.
Over 200+ people.
1 mind.

'Did it help??'
No. It made it worse.

Eventually, I ditched the effort & just focused on spelling
the words. No funny business.

I didn't win the spelling bee that day. Got 3rd place. But
left with a life lesson.

Don't make things more complicated than it has to be on
the public speaking stage.

That underwear advice is cute and all. I get the
rationale behind it. You are humanizing the audience by
indicating to your mind that they are regular people.

But still...It requires conscious effort on your end.
Conscious effort that you should be allocating to the speech.

Same with advice like:
-'Look at the top of their heads.'
-'Look at the back of the room.'

That kind of stuff doesn't work. Even if it does, it won't
work optimally at scale.

'Then what do I do?'
Just talk to one person at a time.

I know you see a crowd. But it's just
INDIVIDUALS sitting next to each other which gives
the illusion of a crowd.

See individuals, and you'll realize you public speak all the
time.
It's called talking.

Fundamentals, my friend. Public speaking is only
complicated when you stray away from the fundamentals.
Forget all the gimmicks.

Remember, one person at a time. Then when you lock eyes
with that person, imagine you are talking to the most
important person in the world.

The beauty?
People around that person will think you are talking to
them as well!!

Multiple birds.
1 stone.

HOW TO BE A DOG

You ever played Monopoly?
'Yes, plenty of times.'
Remember how there was a place called Boardwalk &
Park Place?
'I do!'
I lived in 2 neighborhoods as a child.

One was called Boardwalk. The other was called Park
Place. This was in West Palm Beach.

By the time I moved from Boardwalk to Park Place, there
was a puppy in the house right next to me. Always barking
away. I found it really annoying.

The house had a small white gate around it. So the puppy
would sneak its head under the gate to bark at me. I used
to try to play basketball in my front yard and found it hard
to concentrate with all the barking.

Wished that the puppy would just shut the fuck up!

One day, I missed 10 shots in a row due to all the barking
& was fed up. I went in front of the puppy & started to
make it mad. I started dribbling the ball right in front of it.
The puppy tried its best to wiggle out of the gate so it
could chase me.

After a while of clowning the puppy, the owner suddenly
opened the gate.

'Hey kid, get out of here & stop messing with my dog!'

This got me scared & I ran.

I was 8 years old at the time.

Nowadays, I think about why the puppy acted like that.
Why bark incessantly?

It's because the puppy would one day grow to be a dog.

Animals have a luxury that we don't.
'Which is?'
They don't have to think. They live in the present moment.

A human's biggest weapon is also their biggest liability.
'Which is?'
Their intellect.

The intellect is used to dissect & think. Great powers have
been developed with the intellect. We have used it to
leverage logic in arguments, fine tune & execute the
process of elimination.

However, bad things have happened with the intellect. An
example is analysis paralysis.

Analysis paralysis in a nutshell is when the intellect cannot
be turned off at will. The victim of analysis paralysis is
thinking too much & not enough doing.

A human can also become a dog. By that, I don't mean to
get on 4 legs and act like a buffoon. Instead, I mean to
unlock the fire within.

Dog's think less & do more.

Especially in the beginning stages.

In the beginning stages of any craft, it's wise to learn *just enough* so you can begin. Go in with that intention.

If you don't go in with any intention, then you will be like, 'let me just read one more blog, so I know that I have all the information.'

Spoiler alert: you never have all the information.

Let's say Pratik wants to learn how to shoot a basketball. Then Pratik should watch 3-8 videos on how to shoot a ball. Each of those independent videos will have a few concepts being repeated.

That's the core of the subject.
The stuff that matters the most.

Once Pratik finds the core, he goes on to practice the knowledge. That doesn't mean that Pratik stops learning. He continues to learn. But instead of only consuming, he now practices & takes action as well.

He is the dog that doesn't mind making a fool of himself.

On one of my early YouTube videos, I was learning how to use a video editor. Apparently, you're not supposed to edit when the video is being exported. Well, I didn't know.

By the time I upload the video, I am frozen for the first 20 seconds with a goofy ass face. I didn't learn about this error till a subscriber bought it to my attention. After I saw it, I was embarrassed. A lot of people had watched it.

Thought about taking the video down. It would have been easy to delete the video from YouTube & re upload it. But something in me told me to keep it up.

'Why? You're looking like an idiot.'
I know.

No clue why my gut was telling me to keep it up. But I listened. After some time, I understood why my gut was telling me to keep it up.

'Why?'
It was so I could learn to be okay with embarrassing myself & continuing regardless.

A few weeks later, I was going to record a video in a park that was empty. I felt it was the perfect opportunity to record.

By the time I was midway into the video, there were a group of kids who randomly came to this isolated park. They were all watching me shoot this YouTube video, giggling away.

A part of me was like, '*Stop recording. Turn it off & go somewhere else.*'
However, the dog side was like, 'finish.'

Even to this day, anyone who watches my YouTube videos know that I don't edit out anything. From the very beginning to the very end, I just continue. Even if a word is fumbled. Editing out bad parts makes me dependent on technology. The dog side in me doesn't want that.

I had no clue that small mistake with the frozen video would set up a theme for my life.

These are small examples of what it means for a person to discover a hidden side to them. A side which takes action & is okay with embarrassment while starting a new venture.

The embarrassing lessons somehow click later. But being comfortable embarrassing yourself is difficult.
Especially with the fear of judgment.

That puppy did not remotely care that I found the barking to be annoying. It just barked more.

People don't care about you as much as you think. They are contemplating about themselves most of the time. Unless you did something to directly harm their ego, then their thoughts are centered around themselves. Me keeping up that idiotic video was not necessarily harming anyone.

However, it was giving me access to the soft skill of building thick skin.

Early on, it was painful looking like a jackass in front of others. Nowadays, in the field of storytelling, I feel more well equipped to experiment and follow my heart.

Other fields? That may be another learning experience. Surprisingly, all of us have this hidden side to apply.

The side where the desire for greatness beats the fear of embarrassment. Embarrassment is good because it serves as a feedback loop & powers you up in iterations.

Embarrassment should be somewhat tactical. Putting on clown nose & acting like a clown just for the sake of embarrassing yourself does more harm than good.

But embarrassment which is presented when you are chasing a grand goal? A vison?
That's tactical.

This line of embarrassment not only powers you up, but also further validates that others are thinking about themselves.

The dog does less theorizing and does more doing.

Life Irony:
Action teaches the theory better than the theory teaches the theory.

A well-versed dog will realize this.

WHY STORYTELLING IS A FORM OF ENGINEERING

I always wanted to be an engineer. No clue why. It's something that I said I was going to be when I was 5 years old.

Wish was granted.

I remember the first day I became an engineer. The first company I interned for was a small Aerospace company. Since the company was so small, I was able to be much more involved. I was part of a project which was going to give airplane operators a tracking system.

It was amazing to see the product from the idea phase all the way to production phase. I had a behind the scenes look into how many moving parts it took for 1 product to come alive.

But a few years later, things changed.

I joined a big corporation. A fortune 500 company. Now I was a small fish in a big sea. I was still an engineer, but a different one. I was more so the engineer who fixed stuff, rather than create stuff.

That was enjoyable for a few. Until it became boring as
fuck. Felt repetitive to me. But at least I learned
engineering from a different angle.

'Armani, how does all this connect to storytelling?
Hold up champ, I'm getting there.

In this big corporation, I eventually had enough!

I realized how many flaws there were in the system that we
managed. So, I decided to design some PowerShell scripts
to automate the issue. My assistant manager was
hesitant. But my manager was delighted.

My manager had a boss mentality. He liked things being
created to solve problems. He was also disgusted by how
many engineers just waited to be barked an order rather
than be proactive. He decided to take me under his
wing and teach me how to see engineering from the life of
a businessman.

*At that point, I started to see engineering from the life of a
creator, not a worker.*

Now how does that tie into storytelling? Well, at the core
of it all...
Engineering comes down to different components being
structured together to form 1 final product which solves a
problem/s.
  - The components on their own mean nothing.
  - But together, they produce magic.

Same concept with storytelling.

Storytelling comes down to different ideas being structured together to get a narrative across which enlightens the reader.

- o   The words on their own mean nothing.
- o   But when intertwined correctly, it produces magic.

I used to think creative people were weird. My engineering nature didn't like the idea of people thinking of random shit and calling it creative. I thought it was just madness!

When I looked closer, I noticed a lot of creatives operate with frameworks. There was a method to their madness.

That's how the everyday world connects with the storytelling world.

From here on out, see the isolated components. Then comprehend how they all come together to form one final product.

- o   It could be something as simple as observing your remote controller to TV combo.
- o   The different parts in your microwave.
- o   The different apps on your phone etc.

Everything on this planet is a form of engineering.

Practical or artistic.
Just need to read between the lines.

When you start thinking like this, telling stories becomes much easier. Rather than trying to awkwardly push random ideas and rambling away, you become much more coherent.

In a circuit, the battery gives the circuit life.

In a personal brand, you are the battery.

Therefore, get inspiration from the tangible world.
Then turn it into a story in the intangible world.

Look at what a fluid storyteller you are.
Bravo.

WHAT YOUR VOICE SAYS ABOUT YOU

It was 2014. Me & 2 other buddies were studying for our final exam. We were so close to graduating, that this moment felt surreal. But we still had to pass the hardest class in the curriculum.

The other 2 guys with me were Atul & Asif.

After studying for hours straight, we began talking about what we were going to do once we graduated. Atul began talking about his upcoming trip to the Bahamas. He was telling us that he was going on a cruise.

Atul said he was going to check out the shows, eat a lot of food & go jet skiing. It sounded so fun! Atul was normally super stiff, so hearing that he was going to take a trip felt out of the ordinary.

I asked him if he was going to drink while on the cruise ship. Seemed like an innocent question. When I asked Atul this question, he took some time to think about it.

Out of nowhere, Asif explodes.

'Armani, why the fuck are you encouraging Atul to drink? That's not right man.'
Asif began yelling at me.

He started to get all righteous and began lecturing me on the difference between right & wrong. This was laughable considering he was known as the lazy one in our group. It was typically Atul & me studying, while Asif tried to cheat or look for loopholes.

This was the guy lecturing me on ethics??

After a few seconds of his tirade, I told him to calm down & that he was clearly misunderstanding. I never told Atul to drink, just asked him if he was.

After a while, Asif calms down & apologizes. Begrudgingly, I accept. Did I forgive him? No.

For the rest of that meeting, I was saying all the right things. We continued talking about our plans after graduation, discussing the exam, solving practice questions etc. Everything seemed normal from the outside.

Even though I was acting normal, Asif was able to tell that he crossed the line.

He was able to tell without me being confrontational.
'How was he able to tell?'
Because my voice towards him had gotten cold.

The voice is a direct representation of what you are feeling. The tone matters more than the words because each social interaction is an emotional experience, not simply a logical one. It's an interaction of energy.

The voice is the magnifying glass of that energy.

Even though I wasn't verbally abusing Asif, he was able to tell that I was annoyed with him. Why? Because I was angry at him. Those feelings seeped through my voice.

The voice is always communicating signals to your external world. This is exactly why I know so many brilliant engineers who always lose promotions to people less qualified.

They have the facts & knowledge on point. But they deliver their message with so much sharpness, that it takes the warmth out of the communication.

I approach communication skills from a very practical angle. I'm not going to give you some fluff about sounding cheery all the time. I'm simply here to give you awareness.

Your tone is a magnification of your emotion.

Emotion is the color to a painting. Without the color to a painting, you simply got a black and white image. Boring.
- o   The words communicate what's in the head.
- o   The tone communicates what's in the heart.

If you break down what every being has in common, it's the breath & voice.

The voice is your personal brand. It will either serve as a key to open doors or a thorn bush which hurts people.

Voice is often confused with height. What I mean by this is that people make the mistake of the voice being fixed like height.

Setting a New Year's goal to grow 5 inches in your 30s is
a laughable goal. Why? Because it's not possible.

However, setting a New Year's goal to evolve your voice
is not a laughable goal. It's a commendable goal.

'What do the holders of a great voice have in common
Armani?'
They treat the voice like a musical instrument and turn
down their jealousy.

Real recognizes real.

The holders of a beautiful voice allow their ears to respect
the melody of someone else's voice. Broadcasters, great
public speakers, singers. Great voice? It should go noticed.

Appreciate the beauty of their voice. This primes the mind
to think in terms of harmony, rhythm, and melody. No
need to think too much.
'Let's scientifically break down why this voice is so radiant!'
No, that's not needed.

Just allow the ears to be on the lookout.
Learn to see with the ears.

'Do I just look out for other people's voices?'
No, you also look out for your voice as well.

Things that everyone hates:
-Betrayal from a person who they loved.
-Hearing their voice on tape.

Luckily, with information technology, it's easier than ever to hear ourselves on tape. Recorders on the phone, free software on the laptop, podcasting apps etc. How many are seizing the opportunity to hear themselves?

You know how 1 pound of doing beats 10 pounds of theorizing?
'I agree with that.'
Well, 1 minute of listening to your voice beats 10 minutes of listening to someone else's voice.

If you really want to change how you sound, put your money where your mouth is. Or better yet, put your headphones where your ears are.

Talk about life.
Record it.
Listen to it.
Spot which parts you enjoyed.
Spot which parts you can improve.
Rinse and repeat.

Over time, you'll have content material.
Over time, you'll have a beautiful voice.

The voice is not like height. Set the intention to change how you sound, and you will change how you sound. Make no mistake about that.

SECRET TO LIKABLE PEOPLE

I remember a few years ago when I was driving to work, I would listen to the radio. The radio host had this smooth voice & was hilarious. It was mainly his voice which had me listening to him. It had a special aura.

After a few months passed by, I decided to Google what he looked like. When I saw him, I was very surprised.

Dude was ugly as shit! His face did not match his voice whatsoever. But that doesn't matter.

A secret key to likability is having a nice voice.

A voice that attracts people into your world & makes them curious about what you have to say. Getting a voice like that is no easy task.

It requires work, patience & consistency.
Luckily, the voice that a person is born with can be changed whenever they want it to change.

There was this blind voice coach that I heard of a while back. Can't remember his name. He gave me an insight that changed my life.

He said, *'view the voice as a musical instrument.'*

When he said that, it was as though my paradigm had changed. This was genius!

I dumped out my ukulele that day & went all in on
practicing the musicality of my voice.

'How did you practice the musicality of your voice?'
I read out loud & recorded myself.

When I would listen to the audio, I would check how I
sounded. Then, I readjusted.

After a few weeks of practice, I decided to get into
podcasting. Podcasting is one of the best things for the
voice.

After 6 months of consistent practice, I can happily say that
I have improved. This is good news for you because that
means you can improve as well.

Read a book out loud & record yourself or start a podcast.

Just bring awareness to the voice.
'What if my voice sounds icky when I listen to it?'
Everyone's voice sounds icky to them when they listen to
it. continue anyways.

Sharpen it over & over again.
You will improve.

The voice is a musical instrument, and the magnificence is
that you carry it with you all the time!

The voice can either open doors or close it.

PATTERNS

'Armani, why do you talk about communication skills so much?'
Because I need to.

'Why do you need to?
Because it allows me to see how everything is connected.

I always liked looking out for patterns. I think:
Patterns = The universe trying to tell us something.

All around the world, I see patterns.
- o   I see how nature has similarities to electronics.
- o   How electronics has similarities to leadership meetings.
- o   How leadership meetings have similarities to how ants create ant hills.

I used to think the *'if you don't know history, you will repeat history'* quote was bullshit. Thought it was the school system trying to weasel me into learning about history. But nope.

They were right & I was wrong.

When I was not well equipped with history, I thought the people before me were dumb.
'What can I learn from them? They don't have the technology like we do today. The lessons they hold are from the archaic times!' I thought.

But no.

History teaches a ton about human nature. The patterns
that I've been seeing my whole life tie into nature &
human nature.

'What's the difference between a beginner and a master?'
A beginner sees dots.
A master sees a picture.

The picture gives a hierarchy view of what is important &
what is fluff. Leading with the nature & human nature
mindset allows a person to see energy.

*I like talking about communication skills because it helps me see
the picture.*

There are certain communication tactics which are culture
specific. (Think of how different cultures greet each other
differently).

However, there are certain communication tactics which
are human nature specific. It doesn't matter what society or
part of the world you're in:

A laugh is a laugh.
People get angry.
People get back stabbed.

As a beginner, everything looks unpredictable.
As a master, everything is predictably unpredictable.

If you told me a year ago that communication skills are just
like electrical engineering, but on a higher level, I'd
laugh at you. I kid you not, there are a lot of similarities.

'How can I learn about human nature?'
A few ways:

-Learn history.
-See how anonymous accounts talk on social media.
-Observe people when they get drunk.
-Learn from emotions.

When you see the intangibles, it's easy to realize that the world isn't all rainbows & butterflies. Very dark out there.

Luckily, with perspective of where the shadows lie, it is much easier to walk in the light.

MASS

COMMUNICATIONS

Apparently, Plato was not a big fan of the written word. He thought it was dangerous to write thoughts down & not be around to defend them.

He was completely anti-media.

Well, Plato. I'm here to tell you no one gives a shit. No disrespect to Plato, of course.

Mass communication was going to happen at one point of history or another. Humans are wired to spread information.

Mass communication is when a source can send a message to multiple receivers.

The first wave of mass communication was the printing press. Then, it became prevalent to spread messages via air waves. Radio and television became mainstream.

During the era of radio and TV, there were a lot of gate keepers. A group of people who would deem what content was 'appropriate' or 'inappropriate' to spread to the masses.

Nowadays, the gatekeepers are mainly gone. Mass communication is taking on a different era. Limiting beliefs are the only gate keepers.

One of the most important topics never taught was media
literacy. It is the subject of being able to navigate the media
landscape.

Incredibly important skill set in today's interconnected
world.

I saw a picture of the internet recently from afar. It showed
all the node & network connections. From a high-level
overview, it looked like the neural pathways of a brain.

Why is this important? Because nowadays, the exchange
of ideas is rapid. More importantly, Earth is having an
evolution.

The internet nodes are symbolic of neural pathways.
Our world is growing like a baby who is maturing.

Wow.
The world is so connected.

We are no longer just talking at local levels, but
global levels as well.

This is good news & bad news.

Bad news is that now unqualified people have a voice.
Good news is that now qualified people have a voice.

I think the good outweighs the bad.

Watching the trash on mainstream media is cringe
worthy at this point. My prediction is that the world will
be much more well informed.

Still, there is always the Pareto principle. 20% will begin hitting genius levels while 80% will suffer from excessive outrage.

These are just predictions.

With the era of mass communications changing, it crucial to start being more aware. Every message is intended to have an impact. Social media takes up a different role.

The wise will be mindful of their:
-Facebook feed.
-YouTube suggested videos.
-Twitter trends.

All these are clues into building media literacy.

The information you consume is the person who you become. In this hyper connected world, curating is wise.

o   Content = Externalized thoughts.

Content will influence the subconscious mind.
The smart will view content as food for the mind.

THE ART OF TEACHING YOURSELF

When I was in the 4th grade, I remember my classmate & teacher having a debate. They were arguing about which search engine was bigger:
Ask Jeeves or Yahoo.

Yahoo was popping among the students.
So, my classmate was repping her peers.

Ask Jeeves was popping among the adults.
So, my teacher was repping his peers.

After a while of debating, they realized that they were arguing about the same thing. They realized that both search engines ended up accomplishing the same goal.

'And what was that?'
Getting you the right information, which pertains to your life.

Around that time, we had dial up internet. The internet where you had to block off your phones to access it. That feels ancient now that I think about it. We have come far in terms of digital access.

Back then, it was Web 1.0. The internet which wasn't interactive. Most people who used the internet were spectators. They read what was on the sites & that was about it.

With the rise of technology, we created Web 2.0, which is the interactive internet. Nowadays, if you like a picture on Facebook, you can leave a heart on it.

That's you interacting with the internet.

This is the reason why *'there is no such thing as a stupid question'* is a stupid statement. There are stupid questions. Ask enough of them & you'll lower your social value. You'll also damage a lot of opportunities.

'What do you define as a stupid question?'
A question that you could easily Google.

- o Smart question: How was your experience with Toastmasters?
- o Stupid question: What is Toastmasters?

Back in the days, you'd get away with that shit. People would just think:
'Ah, he doesn't know better. Who knows! This poor sucker may not have dial up connection.'

Nowadays? You're just proving to be lazy. Definitions are the first thing you can Google.

Often, you don't need a mentor in the early stages nowadays. (*I am referring to creative fields such as personal branding, blogging, storytelling. For certain industries, a mentor may be smart*).

There's all the information out there for you on Google to consume a little & begin.
'But a mentor will save me time!'

That's a myth.

Mentors save you time when you are in the fine-tuning process. You fine tune once you have gotten experience, developed raw talent & need to sharpen the blade.

But in the beginning, they won't serve much purpose. Sometimes, they can hold you back. They make you dependent & sap away the natural curiosity.

Because as a beginner, you'll be asking beginner questions. A mentor with experience doesn't want to be sitting down answering questions which are:
1. Minuscule.
2. A few Google searches away.

You don't want to 'save' time in the beginning stages. You want to spend time.

I learned public speaking by watching a few comedians & politicians giving speeches, then headed off to a Toastmasters club.

The club offered me a mentor. I declined. I didn't even talk to a mentor until speech 6. That's when I had tapes that I was able to review with him, so I could make the most out of his suggestions.

This is the era to teach yourself & apply.

The more you apply, the more strategic you will get on how to navigate the internet to supercharge your skills. The more experience that you gain, the more laser targeted your

questions become. The more laser targeted your questions
become, the more you step back from asking others, and
instead, ask yourself.

This is when you truly maximize Web 2.0.
'What do I begin doing?'
You start becoming a creator.

Back in the days, most of these people were spectators of
the internet.

Nowadays, the top dogs in any field can contribute & build
their own stuff. There is a niche out there for anyone.

The best brands are built from hobbies.

'What if there is not a niche for what I want to talk about?'
Then make it yourself. This is more time-consuming. But
in my eyes, well worth the wait.

When I got on Twitter & YouTube, no one was
consistently contributing on topics about storytelling &
public speaking. So let me start one. And I did. No reason
you can't start one too. Digital real estate compounds over
time if you got some hustle in you.

It all comes down to teaching yourself what you are
curious about. Once you find what you're curious about,
that's when learning becomes fun.

1. Gain experience.
2. Once experience is gained, you realize that you can learn
from anyone when you have the right lens.
3. Begin contributing in some way.

That's how you teach yourself in the new era.
Being a bystander is easy.
But it's not fun.

If you want to have fun, then you need to jump into the
battlefield and make your mark. Those are the people who
will engineer everlasting brands.

THE POWER OF SMILE

It's hard to be worried and happy at the same time. Often, it's one or the other. A lot of worrying comes from focusing on what's out of our control.

An example is with the newbie speaker. Constantly wondering if the audience will like them or not.

If this speaker focused on having fun, then things would change. They would feel more relaxed. The relaxation would allow the creativity to flow.

This is where the smile comes in.

'What does it mean to have fun?'
This question was difficult for me to answer.

I didn't know what 'fun' meant.
I knew the definition.
But what was it specifically??

After thinking about it for some time, I finally had a lightbulb moment:
Fun can only happen during moments of not fearing judgment.

That's when relaxation happens. That's when the internal fire is lit.

My laptop background is of a cartoon character staring at the universe. No clue why, but it makes me feel *relaxed*. It opens up my mind and it allows me to have my definition of 'fun.' I don't fear judgment when I see how small I am in the grand scope of things.

Why I have a picture of the universe on my laptop may make o sense to you and that's fine. We all have fun in different ways. Sort of like a thumbprint or our personalities.

'Can we unlock relaxation at will?'
That's where the smile comes in.

I think we are sleeping on the smile. I think this simple move has the power to change our lives.

Holding a smile releases endorphins in the brain. Endorphins are feel good chemicals which help you feel relaxed. Charles Darwin created the smiling feedback theory a while back.

The theory states that when you are happy, you smile.
When you smile, you are happy.
An ongoing loop.

This is the ultimate cheat code when you are nervous.

Back to that newbie speaker who keeps wondering if the audience will like him or not. His anxiety is hitting the roof.
It's hard to relax in those circumstances. Or is it?

Stand up straight and smile, newbie. It will work wonders.

You can't always control your thoughts. But you can
always control your body. Fortunately, controlling your
body leads to thoughts which are in your favor.

That sounds like fun to me.

THE FREQUENCIES OF INTROVERTS & EXTROVERTS

I was sitting in the airport. More specifically, in the airport lobby waiting to get on board.

As I sat in the lobby waiting, I noticed **2** gentlemen interacting. One was an open body languaged, loud, animated fellow. The other one was sharp in their movements, softer tonality & less animated.

Watching both of them interact was fascinating.
'Why?'
Because they were socially rigid.

Both these **2** fellows were stuck in their ways. Not a lick of dynamic movements from them.

The loud fellow was being loud. The reserved one was rolling his eyes & taking his time to respond. The amount of time it took for the reserved person to respond was now annoying the loud person.

Results?
The loud person was now rolling his eyes too.

If you listened to the conversation based on words, everything would have seemed fine. But if you analyzed the interaction with your eyes, then the story was vastly different. The interaction was awkward as hell. The entire vibe was not pleasant.

What is vibe?
Vibe is short for vibration.

Vibration is the language of the social dynamic's world.

When interacting with another human, it is not the words that matter as much as the vibrations that are sent out.
   o   Words communicate to the conscious mind.
   o   Vibrations communicate to the subconscious mind.

The latter is what makes a social interaction pleasant or awkward.

The vibrations include:
   o   Tonality.
   o   Body language.
   o   Eye contact.
   o   Attentiveness.

All these lead to emotions in the other person. The emotions that are generated by their subconscious mind will be analyzed by the conscious mind.

If the analysis reads pleasant, then they would like to see you again. If not, then they will dart the other way when they see you next time.

People are different.

I'm not a big fan of using the terms introvert & extrovert because I am a firm believer that personality is dynamic

based off moods. But I will use it for the purpose of this
lesson.

By factoring in that people are different, it is easier to
switch the vibe at will.
'Does that mean to be fake?'
Nope!

Keep the same authentic message. But deliver it in a
different way.

- ○ *If you see someone is a tad bit reserved with their body
  language, dial it back.*
- ○ *If you see someone is darting their eyes, squint your eyes to
  come off as less threatening.*
- ○ *If you see someone is mainly a talker, listen more.*

Match their vibrations so you **2** are on the same frequency.

'Can extroverts & introverts be best friends?'
Absolutely. But it requires at least one of y'all to be
dynamic.

The mind dictates the vibe and the awareness dictates the
mind.

Now that you are aware, it'll be easier to avoid making the
same mistake as the **2** dummies from the airport.

GOSSIP

Gossiping seems like a universal thing. Whether you're
located in the East or West. Before ruling it off as a
malicious act, it's wise to find the root cause.

When multiple humans do something without being taught,
that means it's not a surface level act, rather, a deeper one.

Why do people gossip? I think I have an idea.

There are 5 core human desires:
1. *Desire to learn*
2. *Desire to feel*
3. *Desire to acquire*
4. *Desire to protect*
5. *Desire to bond*

Gossiping targets desire 1 & desire 5 with a side of desire 2.

- Desire 1: When humans share information with one
  another, they are giving intel. In this context, they
  are learning about other people.
- Desire 5: It's an act that surprisingly bonds people
  when both parties are participating.
- Desire 2: When a human is learning & bonding,
  they feel pleasure.

'Do you think our past ancestors gossiped as well?'
To a certain extent, yes. Which is why we care about
opinions. It's because being ostracized from your tribe back
in the days was equivalent to a death sentence.

I'm fairly sure the opinions were relayed via gossip. Not sure how they would do it, but this is just a theory. To add onto my theory, gossiping is a primal act that many people didn't grow out of.

'Wait, you think it's a primal an act??
Yes, here's why...

Back in the days, our primal ancestors didn't have books or the internet to learn from. So how did they meet the core desire of learning?

I think it was from talking about good hunting spots & communicating about the other tribe members.

As society evolved, language was created, the printing press was invented & books were designed. Nowadays, rather than gossip being one of the predominant pieces of information, there were other knowledge sources out there.

There was an evolution going on in the mind. Some adjusted, many didn't. Survival of the fittest, *intellect style.*

I don't think all gossip is bad. Sometimes, you need to bring up certain people to illustrate a point or concept. The problem is when that's the only subject matter a person is comfortable expressing.

There was the famous quote:
"Small minds talk about people. Average minds talk about events. Big minds talk about ideas."

I think that's spot on.
However, the big minds were not always able to talk about ideas. They had to work their way up.

Ideas aren't something that you just slap together. Highly intricate web of concepts, critical thinking & stress testing leads to an idea.

A big reason why friends grow apart is due to the differences in subject matter of their conversations. Some friends can align their conversation material every now and then.

Other friends are growing into opposites. Although their hearts still connect. Their heads are now different. I'm not making fun of anyone. We may have a few loved one's who only know how to gossip.

Therefore, it's important to understand the primal nature of this act, so we don't immediately deem them as a second-class citizen.

Interpersonal skills come down to the realization that we can't change someone. Especially someone who sees nothing worth changing.

There is good news.
We can change ourselves.

It's never too late to graduate into a big thinker. A thinker who creates ideas and discusses them. Lead by example & others will one day follow. Even those who seem beyond saving.

STORYTELLING MARKETING

I used to hate those popups that would keep coming up when I would go on the internet. It was chaos. Especially a few years back.

By the time ad-blockers came in, the browsing experience changed. I could finally enter the internet without a bunch of spam. Pop ups no more.

A few years later, I met this one affiliate marketer. I asked him how he markets? He said through pop ups.

I was mind blown. I thought ad blockers had killed off popups for good! But that wasn't the case. He was a global marketer.

There were many countries where popups were just getting started. I asked him if he enjoyed what he did for a living.

'Honest truth?' he asked.
I said, *yea, I want to hear the truth.*
He said 'no' in a sad tone.

This was surprising to me. This marketer was making over 5 figures a month with his affiliate marketing style. I wondered why he was so blue.

He said, 'I feel like a nuisance. I have become one of the people that I used to despise. It's good money but something feels wrong.'

I knew how he felt.

I used to sell 30 oz tumblers on Amazon before it was cool. The only main competition was Yeti. During that time, the money was good. Heck, it was great.

But once other sellers got news of the hot product, they began flooding the market. My business partner and I could have fought the good fight. However, that tumbler business had us feeling empty.

There will probably be a few stages when you are only in it for the money. That may help you with the leaps in the beginning. But later?

I don't know, something about the human spirit needs creativity.

The reason the affiliate marketer hated the popups was because he wasn't building diddly squat. The money was there. However, the spirit wasn't satisfied.

"Spirit without material is expressionless. Material without spirit is motionless."

He was a motionless fellow with heavy pockets.

The fix to all of this is storytelling. I'm sure you have heard of content marketing several times before. What exactly is content?

Content is information that is valuable. But what is valuable??

You provide value anytime you target one or more of the desires of another human & elevate that desire.

If you have a strong itch on your back & couldn't reach it, then imagine if someone scratches it for you.

They just gave you value.

    o   Value = Spot target desire -> Elevate desire.
With storytelling, how do you know the desires of a scaled audience?

Say you have 10,000 subscribers. It's almost impossible to know all their desires and talk to each one of them. In this case, flip the spotlight to yourself.

Analyze your desires & write stories about that.

The best way to become a storyteller is by turning your own life into a story. What are your desires & passions? Talk about that. That's the most authentic perspective.

With marketing, you need to bring awareness to something. Typically, it's an offer.

'But what if I am new & don't have any offers?'
Then bring awareness to your brand.

A brand gets an icky perception. While it's simply a construct of perception. Your brain likes to organize data to avoid overthinking information.

Picture trying to imagine all the products that Coca Cola has ever produced. The big liter sodas, the small cans, the polar bear commercial, vanilla coke etc. The brain would explode!

Luckily, the brand of Coca Cola compartmentalizes information.

Even if you don't have anything to sell, then use it as an opportunity to build the brand.

Add content to your website.
Create videos for your YouTube.
Most importantly, learn to become a storyteller.

A lot is changing in the world as of late. Not everyone wants a digital presence. However, it's almost foolish not to at least learn how to leverage a computer/internet in case of an emergency.

Not only leverage a computer for technical work, but for creative work.

A computer is your servant. Instead, many people treat it like their master.

This is the time to be productive.
To be the artist.
Create stories & practice the art.

If you want a brand, blog, YouTube down the line, then go for it. Just make the focus to learn the art of storytelling. Many companies are going to keep bringing up the art of storytelling in the next few years.

It will continue to be one of the hottest topics in the
information age. Get a head start.

Spot your desires & write valuable information around it.
No need for a mentor when you can mentor yourself.

REMEMBERING KOBE BRYANT

Around 16 years ago, I was on a flight to New York. The seats had TVs on them. Excellent! I would have something to watch.

As I was scrolling through the different channels, I noticed a basketball game was on. It was Los Angeles Lakers vs Philadelphia 76ers. Decided to watch it.

As I was watching it, I noticed the 76ers were whooping the Lakers. They were up by 20ish points.

And there was Kobe Bryant.
Giving it his all for the Lakers.

He dropped 40 points that game. 40 points knowing that he wasn't going to make the playoffs.

This was the dark period of Kobe Bryant's career.

A few years earlier, he was on top of the world. He had come off 3 back-to-back championships. Was seen as the heir apparent to Michael Jordan and was simply untouchable.

Now?

Shaq had been traded to Miami. Kobe was labeled as selfish. His Lakers team was not making the playoffs or barely passing the first round.

That period of Kobe Bryant's career is what inspires me the most about him.
The dark years.

NBA has some of the finest talent nowadays.
Unfortunately, a lot of these players lack heart.

Being in that airplane & watching Kobe put it all out there for a game that would have o impact on his season was surreal. Whether he won or loss, the Lakers record was so bad that the playoffs were out of the question.

Still, that fire was what set him apart from many others. That fire was what showed that he was legendary.

4-5 years later, the sun had risen once again.

Pau Gasol had entered Laker land; the organization made some great trades & BOOM!! Lakers were back in the finals.

Kobe ended up finishing his career off with 5 championship rings and he was able to do it his way.

With his first 3 rings, people doubted his greatness.
-They said Shaq carried him.
But with another 2 rings from 2009-10?
-Now he was immortal.

The more you watch sports, the more you can get attached to 1-3 certain players. From different games. We don't just admire them for how they carry themselves on the court. But more so, off the court.

The mindset of a winner is integrated far into their psyche.
It's a game of factoring in discipline & showing up no
matter if it is dark or light outside.

One thing I realize as I mature is that everything comes in
waves.
One minute, you're on top of the world. The next minute,
you're struggling to stay afloat.

People respected Kobe because he always played like he
was trying to stay afloat. Even when he was winning back-
to-back championships.

The key to ambition is always framing yourself as the
underdog, no matter how high you rise.

Kobe Bryant is a winner to the core. He needed to struggle
to show the world what he was truly made of.

Rest in Peace to the Black Mamba.

EMBRACING THE STRUGGLE

Everything comes in waves. From the social circle to our own social media follower count. It's a part of the game.

Another thing that comes in waves is our relationship with certain friends. One moment, y'all are close as hell. The next moment, you guys are doing your own thing. That's just the nature of the game.

If you guys were good friends from the beginning, then when you do realign again, nothing is awkward. Just picking up right where you left off.

I have a friend like that. We are cool for a period. Distant for a period. Then cool again.

The last time I talked to him, we were in different parts of our life. Our political beliefs were 100% different. Couldn't agree on any of the same entertainment and the conversations felt dry.

One of the parts that stuck out was a conversation where we talked about struggles.
-What's one of the worst things that have happened in our lives?

That was a question he seemed stumped on. I could see why.
- o He married his high school sweetheart.
- o Got hired full time from his internship.
- o Bought a house.

Everything was working out dandy.

When asked about his struggles, he said the hardest thing was getting a C in one of his college classes.

I was expecting a heartbreak, death of a loved one, getting fired, going broke etc. Something like that. Nope, it was the C.

I looked at this friend.
He looked soft.

Fat & pudgy. Highly opinionated about the latest topics that the mainstream media hand selected to outrage the public. All that stuff. We are definitely in different stages at the moment.

Time elapses....

Then we catch up once again. Saw him post a video of his wife going through a serious illness & giving an update on Facebook.

She's going to be okay.
However, it was a pretty serious issue for the past few months.

Reached out to him and now he seems like a completely different person.

He seems more rugged.
Less soft & more battle tested.

Apparently, his wife was on the verge of death. Him and his family kept it silent until everything was sorted out.

During that time, he got a peak into a new world. He was having his personal rock bottom and it wasn't just getting a C in some college class.

Struggles mature people and struggles build bonds.

It's hard to connect with someone who hasn't felt pain. Something about the conversation just feels surface level.

All gossip, whining & what is going wrong.
o gratitude.
o depth in ideas.

It takes someone to go through a personalized rock bottom to realize something.
'What?'
We do not only go through one rock bottom, we go through many.

Each new one doesn't feel like a rock bottom because the prior one left us tougher than before.

My friend got a wakeup call. This wakeup call matured him at an exponential rate. Now he is a completely different guy than he was before. It's because emotional pain awakens the subconscious mind. The mind responsible for 95% of reality.

Embrace the struggle. Because ultimately, struggle is simply a word that is put on a human experience.

TAKING THE HIGH ROAD

When I was younger, I always needed to have the last word. Needed to let others know how 'right' I was.

Nowadays, I realize what a poor mindset that was and what a draining mentality it could compound into.

Recently, I had this man getting into a debate with another person on one of my blogs. He was spewing a whole bunch of nonsense.

The man who was spewing the nonsense was writing big block paragraphs about who knows what. You could tell that he was pretty emotional. While the other levelheaded guy was trying to talk some sense into him with small succinct points.

I briefly read the emotional guy's posts & could immediately notice the fault in his logic.
It was so faulty, that it was almost embarrassing.

Younger me would have needed to jump into the post with a response letting him know how wrong he was.

Nowadays, it's different.

I read a bit of his block paragraphs. Closed my phone and went about my day.

'Why the mentality flip? Why take the high road?'

Well, for me, it was not taking the high road. It was taking
the normal road.

When I was a little kid, I didn't have anything else on my
plate. My schedule was too free. Which made it extremely
easy to get caught up in little back & forth's like this.

When you lack any kind of purpose, you get sucked into
these random tasks mistaking it as productivity.

When you have a semblance of a purpose along with a
schedule that requires you to show up, taking the high road
becomes easy.

I sometimes wonder how anyone has time to write these
big block paragraphs on the internet. But then again, it's
probably because they don't have much else to do. So they
confuse their back & forth's as "making a difference."

- o   An argument is all about **WHO** is right.
- o   A discussion is all about **WHAT** is right.

Unless I'm getting paid to change someone's mind, then
I'll let them think whatever. That's my personal
philosophy.

The more comfortable you are with letting someone think
whatever, the less you identify with opinions.

Old school me would have felt strong physical sensations
letting this guy off the hook so easily.

Which is why letting someone think whatever they want
requires a lot of restraint. Emotional impulses need to be

tamed to show **EQ.** That restraint is a workout for the internal world.

Sort of like your inner body is lifting weights. The more weights it lifts, the thicker the skin. The thicker the skin, the less the stress.

A byproduct of thick skin is more creativity. Plus, creativity is the hottest commodity in the age of the Internet.

Taking the high road will have you feeling like you are losing the battle...
All to figure out that you have won the war.

If it's extremely difficult to take the high road, then it may be a time to look at the mirror. There is a reason you keep getting sucked into petty shit.

You can never get to your destination if you get distracted by every dog that barks.

It's the nature of the dog to bark. However, it's the nature of the winner to move forward.

CHIEF STORYTELLING OFFICER

It came to my understanding that nowadays, companies are looking into a position called:
CSO - Chief Storytelling Officer.

If you were to tell me this would be a position a couple of years back, I don't know if I would have placed much importance on it. Nowadays, it has my interest.

A couple of years back, I was doing my master's in Business Analytics & Information Systems.

During my classes, I would hear that the hottest position one day would be:
CIO - Chief Information Officer.

That made a lot of sense to me.

It wasn't too along ago since big data became a thing. Due to the rise in technology & storage spaces, companies given data on their customers like never before.

Companies knew the buying patterns of their customers, their customer's background, what they were saying about the company's products on social media etc.

The next question was, *so what?*

All the data doesn't mean anything without meaning. Data without meaning is like bricks without cement. You just got a bunch of junk.

Structured Data = Information
You can have data without information.
But you cannot have information without data.

So as big data & artificial intelligence grew, it was obvious that information officers would be needed. The CIO would be required to present knowledge to the higher ups so the business flowed smoothly.

Well, fast-forward a few years to the present day...
And the more 1 write this, the more a Chief Storytelling Officer makes all the sense in the world.

Because think about it.
Structured Data = Information
Colored Information = Story

Imagine you are a big company going to the public with a bunch of information. Now the public will be like, *so what?*

On the flipside, you wrap the information in a story & a segment of the public will find it hard not to listen. We aren't trying to appeal to everyone. A segment is plenty.

It was just a matter of time before a CSO position was born.
The future is transitioning to a creative generation.

The beauty about storytelling is that you don't need to run some fortune 500 company to tell your story. You just need to be the CEO of your own ship.
'And what ship do I command?'
Your life.

If you have a life, then you have human experiences.
  ○ *Data.*
If you have reflection skills, then you hopefully know how to structure those experiences.
  ○ *Information.*

Alright bud, you know what the next step is.
It's about learning to tell your story.

The beauty about storytelling is that it doesn't need to be something grand. You don't need to book out stadiums to market yourself as some storyteller. It is best to keep it simple & to the point.

Just understand storytelling as a:
Connection of ideas.
These 3 simple words give the best insight into defining storytelling that I ever experienced.

When you get in the habit of connecting ideas for long enough, you'll get bolder. More fearless. That's when connections from different fields will occur.

The more stories you tell, the smarter you become.
It's easier to see patterns now.

PSYCHOLINGUISTICS

A few of the most powerful forces in the world are intangible.

2 that stick out are the:
-Mind.
-Voice.

What about the combination of both?
-Psychology is the study of the mind.
-Linguistics is the study of language.

What happens when the **2** worlds meet?
You get psycholinguistics.

Repeated exposure to information can change your paradigm. Words influence your mind & your mind influences your reality.

But let's start at the beginning... Take a walk down memory lane. Think about the first memory that you can possibly remember. Take your time.

Once you spot that memory, how are you remembering the information?
'In pictures.'

If I ask you to share the information with me, how will you do it?
'With words.'

At first, when you try explaining it in words, you are going to have difficulty. Mainly because the memory was from so long ago. Your sentences will be choppy.

If I give you a week, you will be able to explain it more clearly. You'll begin to notice something.

The more you use words to explain those memories, the more clarified the memory becomes.

Language is playing a role on the mind.

Since growing up, reality was shaped with words. You were given words which represented a portion of reality. Sort of like how math represents reality.

There are not actual entities of 1, 2, 3, 4 running around. Rather, 1, 2, 3, 4 are concepts which help us explain the real world.

If someone is holding some apples, you will use the number 4 to represent the amount they are holding. The number 4 represents a portion of reality.

Which is why communication skills are not only a way to build influence with others.
It's a way to build influence with yourself.

Gotta' use the right words when you are talking to yourself. The right words are turning into pictures for your brain which is shaping the narrative.

Neuroscience 101:
-The brain influences the mind.

-The mind influences the brain.

Everything that you have been learning, doing & thinking about has shaped neural pathways in the brain. Those neural pathways create an emergent property which is the mind.

The beauty is that you can use that mind to now rewire new neural pathways to your brain. Pretty cool when you think about it.

Intelligence was never fixed. It was more of a lifelong process.

With the surge of technology, we can do more research on the brain. As we do more research, we can see that the brain is able to be shaped.

It's a process called neuroplasticity.

Practice psycholinguistics for life. Not as scary as it sounds. It's just about choosing your words more carefully and being more mindful of the words you consume. Even though you cannot tell, your brain is picking up on small things. Don't need to over analyze this one.

When you are afraid of doing something, just practice reframing.
  o   Reframing = Changing the narrative.

Wrong: I have to give a speech.
Right: I get to give a speech.

These small tweaks add up. It reprograms the brain over time. The language will shape new neural pathways on the brain and the new neural pathways will lead to a renewed mind.

*In return...*The enhanced awareness of the mind will use language more strategically. The brain will level up further.

That's the power of words.

Embracing the world of communication skills has the power to shift reality.

CAN BIASES BE LEVERAGED?

It doesn't take a rocket scientist to see the overwhelming bias in the mainstream media. Some of the news outlets take pride in their bias. They use it to zone in on their target audience. For other media organizations, it tremendously hurts their credibility.

Question is: Can biases be avoided?

Depends.
'Depends on what?'
It depends on many factors. But predominantly on the scale of the organization.

Let's say an organization has 1-3 people.

Then it's not too difficult to tame the bias which rears its head. This small group can talk it out & the parties involved can all agree on reasonable terms of what constitutes as bias & what doesn't.

However, as the organization scales (as all mainstream organizations do) bias goes from being a black & white issue into a gray one. What I consider bias may be considered fair for you & vice versa.

In a perfect world, the news organizations would cover the facts & let us make up our own judgement. But we do not live in a perfect world. We live in a world which are controlled by flawed humans.

As repulsive as bias may be for mainstream media, I want
to share an exclusive insight with you.

'What is that?'
Bias is great for content creation!

Picture a writer's content that you resonate with. This
writer is someone who speaks to you.

Chances are when you are reading this writer's content,
you are not solely looking for pure statistics. You can just
Google the statistics yourself.

'Then why I am resonating so much with this writer?'
Because you want their real-life experiences & key
takeaways.

Surprisingly, the inherent nature of bias can be turned into
leverage. My personal biases lean towards victor mentality,
accountability & work ethic. This book isn't for victims &
whiners. That allows me to strategically polarize by
repelling weak minds real quick!

Personal Biases = Personal Branding Narrative
Whether you are giving a speech or sharing a message
online, it doesn't matter. Be real.

In a perfect world, biases don't exist. But we are human.
Therefore, we have naturally ingrained biases from our
experiences, belief systems & viewpoints.

Be fair when you need to be fair. However, when sharing *your* story, my recommendation is to tilt whichever way that your life points towards.

As the old saying goes:
"Turn your mess into a message."
That is how brilliant communicators create content.

ARE YOU TOXIC?

'Don't ask me Armani.'
I have to.
'Seriously, don't ask me man.'
Are YOU toxic?

This is one of the most difficult questions to ask ourselves because our ego blinds us from the answer. Our ego analyzes life through our intentions & analyzes others based off their behavior. Often, those intentions seem right to us, but not others.

People who you consider toxic do not consider themselves toxic.
'How do you know?'
Because I am speaking from experience.

During 2012, I had a good side & a dark side to me.

Good side was that I was becoming a better student (I struggled with tests my entire life) & was making smarter academic decisions. The dark side to me was that I had anger issues.

My logical side was intact, and my emotions were out of whack.

My logical side began to dominate me. My ego began to paint the illusion that others should behave the same way as me.

I'd be shocked when I would see others not acting like a
good logical boy or girl.

- *Why was this fellow whining? Nothing logical about
  that.*
- *Why was that person late? Nothing logical about that.*
- *Same silly mistakes again? Nothing logical about that.*

Seeing others doing what they were not 'supposed' to be
doing would make me mad. So, I'd lecture them, sometimes
yell, or put them in their place.

It was only the right thing to do, you know? I was only
doing this because I didn't want them to whine, be late, or
make so many silly mistakes. My intentions were right.

What began to happen was that people were afraid to make
mistakes around me. They were afraid because they thought
they would be scolded. This led them to walk on eggshells.

Outcome? My friends either distanced from me or cut me
off completely.

At first, I thought it was their loss & knew I could always
get some new friends. Eventually, it came to a point where
people who were very close to me couldn't be themselves
around me either.

At that point, I came to realize that I was the toxic one.

It's been a few years since those toxic days. Since then, I
came back with one major insight:
- Toxic people often have no clue they are toxic.

I was behaving the way that I was because I genuinely
loved the people I would scold.

Otherwise, I would keep letting them make mistakes.
Despite my intentions being right, it was harming their ego.
When you harm someone's ego, you will be viewed as
toxic.

Always approach humans with an emotional eye, not a
logical one. Or you will make the same mistakes that I did.

Are you toxic?

I don't know.
But you may....

It's a game of suspending the act of viewing everything
from your intentions for a second & see how you are being
perceived.

Social skills are the most enjoyable when approached with
humility. Because the same people we are judging may be
the same people who are judging us. The same acts we are
reprimanding may be the same acts we subconsciously
exhibit.

Others may fear you.
They don't want to be scolded.

The angry man piles up bodies of cold shoulders.
Others distance themselves from the angry man.

People have pride.
They don't want to be spoken to like a child.

Toxicity melts away hopefully.
Toxicity will always exist when humility is lacking.

'SOCIALLY DYNAMIC ENOUGH?'

There are many people on the planet who are socially intelligent. I agree. But guess what?

There are billions of people on the planet who are not socially intelligent. They do not know the basics of how to form a friend.

- *How do you initiate contact?*
- *Is this confident or nervous body language?*
- *I introduced myself, now what?*

These are questions that plague so many people around the planet. I sense some doubt in your eyes.
'Damn skippy you do. I don't think this is that big of a problem.'
Then I have a story that I would like to share with you.

ALL-NIGHTER

The year was 2009.
I was a freshman in college.

Had a Calculus exam the next day that I was not ready for. The squad and I were posted up in the library. We were testing each other.

The hours were flying by.

Felt like we were running out of time. Then there was a guy that came and sat down at our table. Let's call him Ralph.

Apparently, my friend invited him to study with us. Okay homeboy. Let's hope your math skills are on point.

OFF TO A SOUR START

Ralph was sitting right next to me. He seemed a little weird. He was avoiding eye contact the whole time. I would ask him questions. He would answer, then look away.

But it didn't end there.

He did not even bother to create conversation with me. I tried a few times to spark something. But nothing. Not a lick of spunk from Ralph.

I was mad.
An 18-year-old me was super immature.
I gave him the silent treatment.

Had no interest in being his friend anymore.
Ralph, you sir, can fuck off.

FAST FORWARD

March 2019, I gave the best man speech for Ralph's wedding.
'What the hell? How? What changed?'
I am glad you asked.

Here's the thing. Ralph was not being an asshole to me at all. He came up to me the next day to apologize for his cold attitude. Ralph told me that he suffers from social AND test anxiety. Being around new people terrified him.

That pain was amplified by the fact that we had a final exam that would dictate 30% of our grade coming up.

You see?

I made an awful error in judgment.
I operated out of my ego.
I failed to perspective shift.
I failed to show emotional intelligence.
And I failed to show social intelligence.

SO WHAT?

Do you see how a misjudgment in reading another person can throw someone off from pairing a social bond? Ralph and I are amazing friends, and we will always keep in touch.

I hope that we maintain a friendship long enough for our kids to be friends.

Scratch that. Ralph is no longer my friend.
He is my brother.

We would never have been friends if he did not explain himself the next day. But you know what? Sometimes the person we misinterpret will not give an explanation.

LEARN FROM MY MISTAKES

For years, I would work by myself. Thought working with other people was just hype. I battled shyness for years. That was only because I did not know how to network. I did not know diddly squat about social dynamics.

'Can you explain what you mean by social dynamics?'
Sure.

Many will give you different definitions of social dynamics. I am going to simplify it.

Social dynamics is being like water when dealing in human interactions.
'Water?'
Yes. Be fluid.

You do not drive your car the same way on every road, do you?
'Nah.'
Then why must you talk to every human the same?
'Uh...'

Most of us talk the same way to shy kids as we talk to talkative kids. I see many guys spitting the same exact line to an introverted girl as they do to an extroverted girl.

That is wrong.

Just like Ralph showed me that day, every person is different. It's time to stop operating only out of our own ego when in a social interaction.

WHAT I HAVE BEEN DOING SO FAR

1. Read 'Social Intelligence' by Daniel Goleman.

I would recommend reading the whole book. If you are short on time, see if you can find a summary. This book will get you caught up with the core social principles.

'Okay, read it, what else do I read?'
That is all for now.

2. Begin applying those principles to your past and present interactions to be more socially intelligent for the future.

This step will require you to do some introspection of your past & present interactions.

Ask yourself:

- o What went right?
- o What went wrong?
- o Why did the conversation go stale?
- o Anything I could have done to level up my charisma?

Find out more questions you can ask yourself. The more curious you are, the better.

That is it.

As you start improving your social intelligence, you can then go ahead and equip yourself with more sociology & psychology knowledge. Read more articles & consume more content regarding social intelligence.

THE RISE OF SOCIAL INTELLIGENCE IS HERE

Emotional intelligence has seen a major rise within the past few decades. Now, we will ensure social intelligence takes a rise. We are going to be the pioneers.

Our school system never taught us.
Society never taught us.
Mainstream culture never taught us.

Better late than never, right?

Socially dynamic enough?
You already know.
Now let's redefine what it means to be socially smart.

ONE OF THE BIGGEST CONVERSATION SINS

Small things add up in the social world. Good or bad.
I wasn't too aware of this when I was younger.

When I was in the 2nd grade, my teacher asked me how I
was feeling about a class assignment and I just shrugged my
shoulders.

She got heated and said:
*'Armani. When I ask you a question, please don't shrug your
shoulders at me. Please respond with words. Otherwise, it comes
off as disrespectful.'*

Disrespectful? Really?? That wasn't my intention. But
okay, lesson learned.

That's why I have a lot of patience with people nowadays.
 'Don't you find having that patience to be difficult? Some
people are so damn annoying!'
Hell yea! I find having that patience to be very difficult.

Often, I mess up & become impatient. Particularly on those
days when I'm dehydrated or on those days where
everything seems to be going wrong.

Then I have to remind myself that a lot of people aren't
doing something malicious towards me because they hate
me. It's simply because they are unaware.

One person who was unaware was my old friend from back in the days. I noticed he had the habit of talking about himself, a lot. I listened to him.

But when I spoke? His eyes would wander around.
'Did he stop listening to you?'
No. That's the very fascinating part.

He pays attention to the tee. However, his eyes just go wandering off. He struggles to keep eye contact.

'So, what do you make of this?'
He was listening. Yet, he felt uncomfortable making eye contact. I was able to pick up on this quirk because I've known him for a while.

But for people who do not know him? They will view him as rude. I wouldn't be surprised if this social quirk has cost him a lot of opportunities.

'Wait a minute Armani. Even if he is paying attention, they'll still view him to be rude?'
Yes.

People are visual creatures.

If the eyes are constantly wandering, the other person will see the wandering eyes & assume you aren't paying attention. Even if you are.

The greatest listener's unfortunately commit this social error. They get disengaged in eye contact when the other person is speaking.

Why the disengagement? Because the great listener feel's ugly when looking at the other person. They feel vulnerable.

This is a tough issue to resolve because awareness is the fix. Awareness comes down to spotting the uncomfortable feeling and allowing the mind to let the body know that everything is okay.

Even when the discomfort is there, try to push through it. This is one of the fields where no effort goes to waste.

Looking just **2** seconds longer than your past interaction will lead to monumental changes in the future. You don't have to be confident to begin, but you have to begin to be confident.

Wandering eyes are a distraction.

It'll be a shame if all your great listening efforts are going unnoticed because it looks like you stole something.

You know...
When a thief is looking all over the spot because he believes that he is being suspected?

Let me reiterate.
Eye contact is one of the fields where NO effort goes wasted.

2 seconds longer on the eye contact hold feels like hell now. Fortunately, those **2** seconds are an investment into a heaven on earth in the future.

WHY SOCIAL AWKWARDNESS & CHARISMA ARE A MYTH

In college, there was a semester when there was a new kid named Terin transferring to my school. One of the members from my friend group could not stop talking about Terin.

'Guys, wait till you meet Terin! He is one of the coolest guys you can meet!'
The guy saying this was typically a hater.

Eventually, Terin moved to Tampa & a lot of people from my friend group began chilling with him. For some reason, I always happened to have class when they were all hanging out.

Soon enough, everyone from my group was like, *'Terin is so cool Armani. You two need to meet.'*

Finally, one day, I ended up going to a party where Terin was going to be. By the time I met him, I was a little surprised.

We both looked similar. Same height, similar fashion style & same haircut. That must be why everyone thought we needed to meet.

We finally interacted.

'How did the interaction go?'
Honest truth?

It was so boring! Terin was putting me to sleep.
Mumbled, took forever to respond, low energy and much
more. Why did Terin cause so much hype? I couldn't see
it. At best, he was a normal guy. But nothing charismatic.

I will come back to this shortly.

The next year, there was a kid in my engineering class
named Jesse.

Jesse was one of the smartest engineers I ever met. Genius
level. Only problem? Our class hated him. They thought he
was weird.

Jesse was way too smart. He would sit in the front of the
class by himself & always answer the teacher's questions.
The other kids thought he talked too much.

One day, class had ended & I was staying a few minutes
after to solve some problems. Jesse randomly came up to me
& began a conversation.

He introduced himself & noticed I had asked the professor
a question earlier about semiconductors. Jesse came by to
see if I understood the topic. I told him that I was still a
tad bit confused.

So, what did he do?
He spent the next 2 hours tutoring me.

Jesse was awesome!

He played a lot of sports growing up, studied philosophy, had a business etc. The 2 hours passed on by. No clue why everyone hated him.

These 2 moments made me realize something.

You hear the terms 'social awkwardness' & 'charisma' used often. But both terms are relative.

It is relative to the person using them.

I thought Terin was socially awkward. Others thought he was charismatic. I thought Jesse was charismatic. Others thought he was socially awkward.

What do you consider yourself?
Charismatic or socially awkward?

Want to know something mind blowing?

There are multiple people in the world who would consider you the exact opposite of what you came up with. No one can be liked by everyone no matter how hard they try.

It's like me telling you to go bring me a purple elephant.

You would wave me off as a joke.
But my friend...

You have yet to wave yourself off as a joke despite chasing the impossible task of being liked by everyone.

JORDAN PETERSON

Around 2017, there was this Canadian psychologist who was blowing up:
Jordan Peterson.

When I first heard of Jordan Peterson, I mainly associated him with owning others in debates. He had a mix of brilliance & articulation skills.

There was this debate with him and Michael Eric Dyson. It was my first encounter with Jordan.

Jordan owned Dyson by just allowing Dyson to self-implode.

Dyson made 2 errors in that debate:
1. He pulled the race card too quick & too often, shutting down further dialogue.
2. He used 150 words when he could have used 10.

Jordan's poise allowed his message to become global.

Combine his message with new media & now a star is born. It appeared Jordan came at a great time.

His message of personal responsibility, cleaning your room, developing a life purpose, was great for a lot of individuals who felt lost.

It was refreshing to see a guy encourage responsibility, rather than pushing a victim narrative. His victor mindset lit a fire under many people. The guy who introduced me to

Jordan Peterson was my former coworker who was in his 40s. His daughter had just committed suicide & he said Jordan helped him out of depression.

However, one thing with human nature is that when you are rapidly growing, polarization happens.

Where there is love, there is hate.

Jordan was being called a bigot by another sector of the audience. He took a stance about refraining from using certain government mandated words in Canada, & this caused quite the stir. Also, his stance on the Kavanaugh case had a lot of his own people turning against him. Tough predicament to be in.

2020 must have been a brutal year for Jordan.

In that year, he was going through severe medical problems.

Halfway into 2020, news broke about how his medical problems were life threatening. He was on the verge of death.

After the life-threatening news broke, I thought even the haters would show compassion and wish him the best. Deep inside, it would be wrong to wish death on someone due to a difference of opinions.

But no. That wasn't the case.

There were tons of people who were cheering about his poor health. Pretty creepy if you think about it. Social media can give you a peak into the dark side of human nature.

At the time of writing this, Jordan's health status is a toss-up. As I write this, I hope Jordan makes a speedy recovery. But beyond his speedy recovery, I hope he comes back and continues to spread his message.

He is a bright individual & a highly influential person.

Jordan is unique in the way where he can simplify complex concepts. Meaning, that he is very well spoken. Normally, when someone has high intelligence, they may struggle to articulate their viewpoints.

'Why do smart people find it difficult to articulate?'
Well, not just smart people. People in general.

Unless you take an active approach to sharpening your communication, your speaking and writing will be sloppy.

However, with high intellect, it gets slippery because you are trying to convey grand ideas to others who may not share a similar intellect to yours. The way that Jordan was able to do this without confusing others showcases intricacy.

Still, you know how the mainstream media are. They will get snippets, make the message fuzzy & then stir controversy around that.

Which is why a lot of Jordan's interviews are of him defending himself rather than further articulating his points.

I hope when Jordan comes back, he invests in his YouTube channel and his personal media. His large brand doesn't require him to keep hopping around on mainstream platforms debating in circles.

The problem with someone like Jordan is that his high-level intelligence can rub a lot of people the wrong way. Especially those in the mainstream who have different core beliefs.

When you debate too much with those who have different core beliefs, you create the illusion of progress, while in reality, you are just stirring resentment in the other person.

Human nature isn't always pretty. Double down on the core fans. Make those who like you, love you. Avoid spending time on those who hate you so much. When you give haters time, you make them go from hating you to feeling iffy about you or hating you even more.

Our time won't be returned. Our mind may not age, but our physical bodies sure do. The whole game of fame is an illusion.

Fame is a concept that was created once we developed information technology. Before that, fame wasn't something that was a concern or a gift.

Jordan proved he could go global. Nowadays, if he can expand his message & bring those who already see potential in what he's saying...

Then we may be witnessing something great.

MAKING HABITS STICK

Dropping a bad habit and picking up a new habit is tricky.
It seems easy when learning the theory about habits.
Someone reads a book on productivity and is like:
'Oh, I can do that!'

But there are a lot of challenges that go on behind the
scenes.

One of the toughest things about dropping habits is the
feeling of withdrawal.

The withdrawals take time to lose its energy over you,
especially depending on how much time was invested in
that poor habit.

I had a childhood friend who admitted to being an alcoholic.
I asked him why he didn't just gradually phase it out? The
way I asked the question irked him.

'If it was that easy bro, I would have done it' he
responded.
Then why don't you? I wondered.
Later, he told me.

He feels tremors in his body due to withdrawal.
Uncontrollable shaking.
Can't sleep.
Hallucinates.

The vivid imagery he described sticks with me to this day.
Easing out of a bad habit is no easy task. It's best to never

let it get that bad in the first place. But hey, hindsight is
20/20.

The trick to easing out a bad habit is by replacing it with a
good habit.

Because what are habits?
Repeated movements.
What are repeated movements?
Strengthened neural pathways.

Therefore, how many times the bad habit was repeated will
correlate with the strength of the neural pathways in the
brain.

It's all a game of weakening the pathways over time.
Weakening is done by strengthening the good habit.
Replace one for the other.

'Awesome, thanks! I will get started now.'
Now mind you, this is no easy task.

You may have some moments of relapses as well in your
journey to building a good habit. So rather than being too
hard on yourself, expect it. When you don't expect
something and it happens, it's easy to get infuriated or
scared. When you expect it, then it's easy to be less rattled
when it does happen.

A few years back, I was trying to balance my masters,
business, 40 hour a week job, friends, family etc. My busy
schedule had me picking up the bad habit of only eating fast
food.

As some time went on by, I was gaining weight and not feeling good. But cooking was such a time-consuming process.

What should I do?

I know!
Meal prep.

The goal was to set aside 3 hours every Sunday to cook healthy food for the entire week. That would solve the bad habit of eating fast food.

However, as time went on by, I would sometimes skip those Sundays. Logically, I knew if I missed the Sunday, then the whole week would be doomed to fast food. Emotionally, it just felt good to skip it.

That was my body trying to stay in its old ways. Trying to stay away from picking up this new habit.

The first few times, I became angry. Decided to quit the habit to go back to fast food. Cooking wasn't worth the hassle anyways.

Until later, I realized it was worth the hassle.

If I wanted this new habit, I had to earn it. Neural pathways don't install themselves because you feel like doing something.

It starts with a commitment.

That's why at times, we commit the most after a big scare.
We tell ourselves during the scare, 'if I just have one more
chance, I'm not going to fuck it up this time.'

Then when we do get our new chance, there's hunger.
Our body still tries to fight us.

Yet, the will power is stronger than ever.

Expect that the body will fight you.
It is the nature of the body to feel withdrawals.

The body is persuasive too.
It must've gotten a lesson on sales.
It will try to convince you to turn back to your old ways.

But pick your good habit that you will replace the bad
habit with.

Then put your reps in.

No need to do a lot of hours. That will just give the body
more reason to quit. Just ease out the bad habit by *easing*
into the good habit.

Small steps beat no steps.
Small steps beat gargantuan steps.
It's because small steps lead to gargantuan steps when
consistent.

STIGMAS

I had a childhood friend shoot me a text recently. He had been following my YouTube channel for a couple of months.

I've known this guy for many years. So thought he was going to be making jokes. To my surprise, no. He said he was really interested in what I was talking about.

Asked me if he could call.
I said sure.

He had fallen on tough times and wanted to know how he could get himself back up. Wanted to pick up acts such as public speaking, creative writing, storytelling, and all of that.

He said he wanted to go further by investing into self-improvement, however, he was nervous because his friends associated a 'stigma' to self-improvement.

On Google, a stigma is defined as:
A mark of disgrace associated with a particular circumstance, quality, or person.

Why would anyone associate a tough word like that towards self-improvement? Damn fam, what kind of friends do you have!?

That got me thinking. What doesn't have a stigma?

In my culture, if you became a doctor, you know you made it. If you were not a doctor, then an engineer or lawyer also showed that you made it.

As I started growing up, I noticed stigma's were associated with the fields that I used to view as the untouchables.

I had this one guy who once came in my DM's and asked me if I could retweet a thread of his. He said he had been working very hard on it.

I looked through the thread and the whole thing was shitting on doctors.

He was talking about how doctors are quick to prescribe medicine, make you feel like a victim & are a menace to society. In this kid's world, he had a negative stigma towards doctors.

It wasn't only this kid.

The reason he wanted me to retweet this thread was because it had already gone viral, showing that there was demand for this thread. Over 150 plus people retweeted it, further spreading the stigma of doctors.

As I grew up, I ended up becoming an engineer. I also noticed the stigma's that came from that profession.

Business majors that I worked jobs with assumed that engineers were weird. Nerds, with no social presence or charisma. The 'socially awkward engineer' label is a stigma we hear many times.

One of my friends ended up becoming a criminal attorney.
He said he once got spit on by a woman who called him
a 'murderer protector.'

The lesson is that there are stigmas in anything that we do.

Any field you find, you will find stigma's associated with it.
The stigmas are not intrinsic. Rather, it is a perception that
is assigned by a group of people who do not condone this
lifestyle.

Does that make the stigma a reality?
No.

I couldn't retweet that thread shitting on doctors because I
don't agree with the whole premise of that. For every 150
people who despise doctors, there are 150 people who have
been positively impacted by them.

Same with self-improvement. For every 150 people who
say it's a waste of time, there are another 150 people that
view it as a way of life.

Ultimately, this is why sticking with something long
enough is emphasized no matter where you go.

When you quit too soon, you never allow the vision to
grow up. That's when you let these strangers who you
never met, influence you.

*A lot of time can be wasted because you took the advice of
someone who was hurt & never healed.*

Seeking information is a great habit to cultivate. But for my life, a bigger habit to cultivate has been learning to listen to my experiences & the inner voice who says, 'Fuck what they say. What do you want to do?'

DUAL JEALOUSY

A lot of people you are jealous of are jealous of you too. You'll be surprised by the first time you see something like this happen.

'Why does this happen?'
Because of desires & the 'grass is always greener' mindset.

The ego thrives off lack. It mainly focuses on what it does not have. Mix the multiple human egos in the social landscape with the constant desires, and dual jealousy no longer sounds ridiculous.

It's a case of the successful entrepreneur who is jealous of the unsuccessful entrepreneur's family life. While the unsuccessful entrepreneur is jealous of the successful entrepreneur's business life.

The first time I could recall dual jealousy was in my junior year of college.

During that year, I was the External Vice President of my fraternity. This was the position that would throw events so our fraternity would remain relevant in school. Due to my position, I had the chance to meet a lot of new people.

During that time, one of my college of engineering buddies, Tom, was a bit jealous of all the people I knew. He had just transferred to this school & didn't know many people.

But I was jealous of Tom because of his insane intelligence. He would always score higher than me on engineering exams. Not just by a few points but by a lot more.

One day, when we were pulling an all-nighter for an exam,
I let him know I was jealous of how smart he was. Not in
a threatening way, but in a joking way. He looked
surprised.

'Why?'
Because he said he was jealous of me knowing so many
people.

He had the time to be so good on tests because he did not
have much else to do other than focus on his education.
Tom had been in school for a couple of months & never
went to a college party.

Late night conversations are when personal sides are shared.

I doubt both of us would openly admit to being jealous of
each other had it not been for the late-night atmosphere.

That went onto show that desires shift and the ego can
cause you to be jealous of someone who is equally (and in
many cases, more) jealous of you.

After that incident with Tom, I have more perspective than
I did before.

When we get jealous, we undermine the wins in our life &
amplify the wins in the other person's life.

This causes us to automatically assign ourselves the lower
social value in the interaction. So, we look up to them like
some sort of tittyboi.

When you have an understanding that the other person may be just as jealous of you because you have wins in your own life, the ego does not win.

Instead, you control the ego. There is no assigning yourself a much lower social value.

Obviously, you don't want this to be some sort of intellectual act where you list out everyone you are jealous of, and then follow it up with why they should be jealous of you.

Instead, just level up in your own respective field. This allows for jealousy to be leveraged.

However, leveraging jealousy is an emotionally intelligent act. One that requires taming the ego.

Which is why bringing conscious awareness to other wins in your life settles the jealousy, making it easier to control.

Dual jealousy is a thing in the social world. When you come into encounter with the first dual jealousy moment, it is in an atmosphere when guards are down. When hostility is not present.

Be on the lookout for a dual jealousy moment. Don't seek it. But if it happens, then it happens.

AVOID WORSHIPPING OTHERS

Not too long ago, there was an account who wrote something that I vehemently disagreed with.

It was strange because I normally agreed with most things that this account said. However, for this certain message, it was completely different.

'What was it about?'
That's not the point. The point was that I vehemently disagreed on a message with someone who I normally agreed with.

That's an insight in itself.

'Why do you say that?'
Because it showed me the importance of thinking for myself. Why I should not be lazy and allow someone full control over my mind.

If it was a situation where I worshipped this account, then I would have been in a dilemma.

2 circumstances could have happened:
A. I betray my core principles to agree with the person.
B. I question everything that I learned before from that person.

Since I never worshipped that account, my course of action was no response. Simple.

Now I can continue to learn from the other parts of this account's philosophy that works for me.

That's how easy life can be when you learn to think for yourself.

It's when you have a stronger filtration system. It's all about putting in work now so you can make other courses of action easier later on.

When you get lazy and want others to do full thinking for you, that's when the situation I faced with the account can consume your whole day/week/month/year.

"Gee whiz! Do I betray my core principles or question everything I learned from this fellow?? Decisions, decisions!" you say.

That's not to say that you should never get a mentor. Instead, it's to prevent letting a mentor take hold of your entire life.

In a hard skills field, having one mentor may work. In a soft skills field, having one mentor is not smart in my opinion.
Any field that requires supreme creativity requires for the world to be your mentor.

Storytelling, filmmaking, content creating, poetry etc.
These activities are best when you treat the world as your mentor.

You can learn from animals, politicians, comedians, little kids, business models etc. The creator in you becomes awakened.

When we delve deep into a field, we make a:
1. Logical -> Creativity transformation.
2. Then we become creative.
3. Then we realize logic and creativity were 2 ways of looking at the same thing.

An example is learning how to drive a car.
Logic is required to learn the fundamentals of how the car works.

Once the driver learns how to drive the car, it becomes a creative act. At this point, it's a game of learning how to take new roads, knowing when to turn lanes, when to speed up & slow down using judgement.

As the driver continues to drive, the creative side begins to take charge. The driver realizes that he is still executing the same movements learned in the logical stage, with a creative twist.

That's when the 2 worlds become blurred.

Learning is a process of self-transformation. It's a game of realizing that only the awareness should control the mind.

That's when you prevent yourself from becoming a wierdo as well.

There are certain people who get super agitated when someone they admire writes a controversial opinion.
They zone in on that & let their whole day get ruined.

How peculiar.

Why are you letting a person you never met get under your skin? How free are you when you act like that? That's why social media can show you how unhinged some people are.

On the other hand, groups who learn to think for themselves? The one's who view the world as their mentor? They take what works for them & ditch what doesn't. No more complicated than that.

That's maturity.
That's how the internet was meant to be used.

In the future, the smart will get smarter while the emotionally unintelligent become more clownish.

PLUMMET YOUR LIKABILITY 101

The world is highly interconnected. Poor interpersonal skills can boomerang back.

On one summer day, I was driving to a meeting. As I was driving to this meeting, I noticed it was excessively hot.

Florida is already known for its hot weather, but today was different. 93 degrees & the car's AC didn't seem to be making it any cooler. So, I did what any sane guy would do. I dialed up the AC to full blast.

'Did that help??'
No. Now, it just blew warm air at full blast.

I definitely can't spend the whole day like this. Something has to change.

As a result, I end up going to a local car shop. A car shop that apparently specializes in fixing ACs. I guess a service like this is really needed in Florida.

I go inside and see this gentleman in his 60s at the cash register. He doesn't greet me as I walk in. Instead, he is intently observing something on the cash register.

I stand there in front of him for 35 seconds before he finally looks up and says, 'Yea?'

*Hello good afternoon. Hope you are doing well. My AC stopped
working. Do you guys add freon here?'* I asked.
'Yea, but you have to wait till Saturday.'

Today was Wednesday.

Do you have any other day closer by? I responded.
'Nope.'
'Dang, its super-hot' I said jokingly.
'Not my problem.'

This guy was clearly not the most empathetic type.
I told him I'd get back to him & dipped.

I decided to drive around looking for a different place.
Soon, I found another spot that also specialized in AC
fixing. Parked my car & walked into the office.

'Good afternoon! Welcome to Ice Auto Shop. Is there
anything I can do for you??' a woman enthusiastically
greeted me with. She was in her mid-30s & had a bubbly
personality.

I let her know of my situation & told her what was going
on.

'Oh, I am so sorry sir. But we are so booked. The earliest
I have on my calendar is on Saturday, is that okay?'
I was a little frustrated considering I still had to wait.

'It's really burning out there sir. I understand how you feel.
But we will definitely get you all caught up this Saturday!'

I was frustrated at first. But after her level of compassion, I was not nearly as frustrated as before.

Same wait days for both auto shops. Guess who I ultimately chose to work with? The second person, no brainer.

That is a little story on social skills.

In this story, the gentleman committed **2** big social sins:
1. He lacked enthusiasm.
2. He lacked empathy.

When I entered the office, he didn't even greet me. Very rude way for an employee to behave.

What was worse was how he didn't have the empathy to relate or acknowledge the problem his customer was facing before giving a rebuttal.

The sweet woman was **100%** different. She greeted me in a bubbly fashion & related to my problem before gently offering a rebuttal.

This story is a lesson for social interactions. It really is a game of being able to adjust. More importantly, it's a game of seeing the gray areas of life.

People who are going through a tough day tend to think way more emotionally than they normally would. Emotions are the gray areas of life.

The gentlemen technically said all the right things. Logically, he did well. In terms of emotionally, he lacked

energy & the ability to connect to the person he was
speaking with. Flaws like this will cause a person to lose
favor with someone's good graces and business.

Are you someone who behaves a tad bit too logically?

Then there is a chance you need assistance with social
intelligence.
Aka: street smarts.

When faced with an agitated customer in your life, it's the
sweet woman's attitude that will win. Not the grumpy man
who hates his job.

Street smarts is a game of reading emotions & adjusting at
will. It's a superpower.

With this superpower, the eyes get an **X-R**ay vision.
Compassion beats the tendency to personalize.

A lack of personalization is the hidden portal towards
opportunities, abundance & a magnetization of more
opportunities.

SECRET TRUTH TO NETWORKING

Charisma is a superpower in today's world. Especially with global communications making the world smaller and smaller. Charisma is now expanding into digital charisma. That's a part of the future.

We all have our own unique brand of charisma.

It is not a one size fits all type of personality. However, charisma alone will not get you far in networking. What will get you far is time, consistency & patience.

Networking is the act where you communicate with others with a purpose in mind. Aimlessly gossiping away with someone is not networking.

Networking is when you have an end goal in mind of who you want to become. Then you strategically talk to the right people to make that dream a reality.

Sort of like completing a massive puzzle.

To complete that puzzle, charisma will make it much easier to find the pieces. Charisma will allow you to be personable & someone worth getting to know. But ultimately, charisma will only get you so far.

Finding the puzzle piece alone is not enough. It requires patience to find the right location for that puzzle piece.

In the real world, charisma is not enough. It requires patience to nurture the social bond & build trust to see where the social asset fits.

'Armani, networking doesn't work for me!'
Why not?
'I've been to a few events, showed face & no one ever referred me any business.'

How many events?
'2.'
2???? That's nothing.

You need to be seen multiple times until you are sealed in someone's subconscious mind. Till then, the world is way too noisy to remember someone who went to 2 events.

The asshole who is always seen is more loved than the charismatic person who goes ghost mode. Why?
Because humans love familiarity.

You ever heard the saying: *'He's a nice guy when you get to know him?'*
That actually means: *'He's just an asshole, but you get used to it.'*

This isn't to say that you put your charisma in the closet & start being an asshole. Instead, use your superpower.

Spiderman wouldn't be shit if he had all those superpowers but was fiddling with his balls in front of Netflix all day.

What makes Spiderman special is that he has the
superpowers, and he shows up in the crime to leverage
those gifts.

Use your charisma to make your presence felt.
-Don't just show up & never be seen again.

Use your charisma to build trust.
-Don't just sweet talk & have empty words.

Use your charisma to nurture social assets.
-Don't just give out your card with enthusiasm & dip.

You have a superpower my friend.
Leverage it.

META-COGNITION

In the College of Engineering, the students had to take a bunch of random electives. 2 electives which didn't make sense to me were, 'World Religions' and 'Racism in America.'

Nothing personal against those 2 courses but I was in the College of Engineering. I had no clue how those courses tied into anything engineering related. I thought I was wasting my time.

One day, I went to my advisor and asked him why I was taking those classes. Last I checked, college courses weren't cheap.

His response:
'It's because you are gaining more perspective of how the world works.'

I thought that was a slick response. Thought the advisor was strong arming me into filling his pockets.

By the time I got into my first internship, my mindset had changed. I realized exactly what he had meant. Aspects such as religion played a big role in the creation of an engineering product.

An example was that a lot of our team members were off shored in India. Scheduling a deployment on Diwali would have been in poor taste.

Meta cognition is when you're aware of your own thinking.

Thinking about thinking. Or being aware of being aware.

This is a big tool in the real world because you oversee
your curriculum. No one is telling you which courses to
take.

There are 5 Levels of Communication:
- o   Level 1 - Self awareness
- o   Level 2 - Dialogue
- o   Level 3 - Group interaction
- o   Level 4 - Public Speaking
- o   Level 5 - Media

Meta cognition falls into level 1 communication. Without it,
you may be having your time wasted & be completely
unaware of it.

In school, memorization is rewarded.
In the real world, understanding is.

If you are putting yourself in scenarios where you are
cramming, then you are failing. It means you are showing
poor strategy in information accumulation. Tsk tsk.

'How do I improve?'
You improve by observing your thinking.

One of the best ways to do this is through 'thinking
meditation.'

A common meditation practice is breathing meditation. This
is where you count your breaths. Thinking meditation is

where you just observe your thoughts, completely
uninterrupted. Go where it takes you.

Once you have done this for a few weeks, you have
developed the fundamentals of level 1 communication.

Now when you study, you will understand which areas you
are good in & which areas you lack in. Then, you can
design a strategy to fill in the gaps. Much more effective
than reading random books which have nothing to do with
your vision.

Just consume information which is eventually going to lead
to an output. Everything else is secondary.

The more you practice observing your thinking, the more
metacognition skills improve.

There are a lot of resources out there which will waste
time. Being able to spot garbage information is a skillset of
its own.

Once you begin getting a grasp of your thinking patterns,
you'll see links & patterns among subjects much more
effectively.

You may see how World Religions has a lot to do with
engineering, who knows.

Level 1 communication reflects all other forms of
communication. Invest in level 1 & it becomes much easier
to tackle the other levels.

WHAT EXACTLY IS GRATITUDE?

Gratitude is like a coin. A coin has **2** sides to it. Head & tails.

'Well technically Armani, a coin has **3** sides! Head, tails and the edge.'
Yes, you are correct. But for the sake of the example, let's keep it to **2**.

Even if you like the heads side more, it does not negate the other side being in existence. When you flip a coin, there is always a possibility that the tails side can be the one that lands.

However, most people live life only hoping for the heads. They think all is good when the coin lands on heads and something must be wrong when it lands on tails.

The heads represent the perceptions of the ego and the tails represent the whole picture in this analogy.

- o   When you just hope for **1** side, you get bitterness.
- o   When you accept the whole coin for what it is, you get confidence.

So, what is gratitude?
-Gratitude means acknowledging wins.

What does acknowledging mean?
-Acknowledging means bringing awareness to.

Gratitude leads to an abundance of creativity.
Creativity is when you exit the fear-based mentality &
unlock new perceptions. Perceptions that someone who is
always competing will never see.

Someone who is always competing has the core operating
system of scarcity. They think something is running out.
Some fields require extreme competitiveness like sports, so
that makes sense. However, on many occasions, people
compete on activities that are meant to be lead with a
creative mindset.

Gratitude gives energy. I used to think it was just a mental
act. But the mental & and the physical are connected. Just
like the heads & tails are. Find a way to control one &
you'll control the other.

Gratitude creates a whole person. Being whole is the staple
of confidence and allows you to slow down.

Sooner or later, everything always leads back to awareness,
no matter which subject/skill set you choose to invest in.

Leverage your awareness to acknowledge your wins.
Big or small.
A win is a win.
Count them, collect them & grow them.

BODY INTELLIGENCE

Let's say that you love playing basketball, but you were never formally taught how to play. You just had a basketball & your goal was to get it through the hoop.

Eventually, you got so good that you were able to make a basket with ease. However, your shot was very unpredictable.

A few years goes by, and you meet a former basketball coach. He says you are raw talent but need to get polished up. He says that he can teach you the fundamentals of shooting a basketball. So, the act becomes more predictable.

Your world is shook...Here you were, just having fun. Now apparently, there is a formal study of this field. A formal study that allows you to tie concepts into real life experiences.

There's a famous quote that goes like:
Theory without experience is just philosophy.
Experience without theory is just ignorance.

I realized that when I am dehydrated, I don't feel creative. I couldn't quite explain it.

Later, I found out that dehydration closes your body off and creates a survival state. A survival state leads to overthinking.

So? I wondered.
The purpose of creativity is to think.

Who cares if I am over thinking?

In the book, Power of Now by Eckhart Tolle, one line in
the book stood out:
The mind that is left alone produces monstrosity.

'Whoa, that doesn't sound pleasant.'
 It doesn't sound pleasant at first, until you understand the
meaning behind it.

I realized that I felt the most creative when my mind was
still.

When the mind was still, that's when I was able to
leverage the thoughts which served me purpose and discard
the rest.

'What's the difference between what you just described and
over thinking?'
- o   With over thinking, I am identifying with the mind.
    This makes it harder to select the right thoughts.
- o   With my creative process, I am not identifying with
    the mind. Which makes it easier to select the right
    thoughts.

To take it a level further, I am identifying with my body.
My awareness is placed on my body & that allows me to
observe the mind as a 3rd party observer.

Eckhart brings up this concept as well. He talks about how
the visible part of our body is simply the surface level.
The key is to feel the energy within the body.

He calls this the inner body. The body that has a connection with the higher self.

That's when experience finally met theory.

It's difficult to create art with the mind. The mind thinks in too many dualistic patterns. It's great to edit with the mind, like proofreading.

But to create?
That's the body's job.

There is an intelligence that resides within our body. Hard to explain in words. It's more so an experience.

To get started, just observe your inhaling breaths. See how far it goes within the body till you lose awareness. Then as you exhale, make yourself aware of which part of your body the breath is coming out of.

'Do I have to do the breath, or can I bring awareness to a body part?'
You can bring awareness to anything. The goal is to check for the energy within.

You'll feel it in your core self. If your body starts feeling warm, then you are on the right track.

Once you can reach this state at will, it becomes much easier to detach from the mind.

The mind is a great servant but a poor master. Sort of like the smartphone. A smartphone is a great tool. But over relying on it causes an addiction.

It's a powerful experience that will not only unlock your inner creativity but will make you feel whole as well.

GOOD CHANGE VS BAD CHANGE

You ever had someone tell you that you changed?
'Yes, I have!'
What was your reaction?
'My feelings were hurt.'
Why?
'No clue.'

I ask you these questions to show you that there are 2 modes of thinking to this question.

One group gets their feelings hurt.
The other group feels empowered.

There are 2 kinds of changes in this world. Good change & bad change. How you define it is up to you.

For me, good change equals habits which lead to an enhanced personality. Bad change is no change. You are the same bubba from a year ago. We all know someone like that.

They fit the traditional mold of the popular high school kid who peaked in high school. What a shame.

The reason a lot of socially awkward people become charismatic later in life is because they started behind the game, which forced them to hustle. They were forced to change.

Same reason why a lot of C students whoop A students in the school of hard knocks. The school of the real world.

If someone tells me that I changed, I celebrate, and a lot of people do the same.

Humans with growth mindset understand the effects of habits. Habits serve as a compass for our lives. Habit's compound, good or bad.

It's hard to distinguish a victor from a victim, at first.

If you want a solid filtration system, see how much importance they put on their habits. A victim is sporadic. They are loyal to bad habits & nonchalant to potential good habits.

Victors live & die by their habits & constantly try to hammer in the new neural pathways. It's the micro changes that lead to the big changes. Starting micro is what warms you up for the lifelong race.

Example: A tweet is a seed. The seed is watered into a following. A seed watered even more turns into a brand.

I said earlier that bad change is no change. But that was not fully correct. There is no such thing as 'no change.' Change is just a part of nature.

So even if you try your best to do something every day the same exact way, you will still notice changes. Kind of spooky.

During my final year of the engineering program, I made my day as predictable as possible. Go to school, come home, eat, study and sleep. That's it.

Well, after following the illusion of 'no change' for 1 week, nature woke up.

Out of nowhere, my car got a hit and run one day. Bumper was fucked up. Now my precious 'no change' schedule had changed.

Had to file a report, get insurance information, send my car to a car shop, rent a vehicle & so on.

When you try to avoid change, change finds you and it's normally not the good kind.

It typically comes masked in anxiety. Do you seek out changes that lead to you leveling up? Or does change come knocking at your door filled with busy work?

Seek out change.

You'll be ecstatic when someone says you don't seem to be the same anymore. Good. That was the intent anyways.

INTENTION

There are a lot of laws that are important in the real world. Compound effect, network theory, Pareto principle etc.

However, there are few laws as important as the Signal to Noise ratio.
-Signal is the meaningful information in your life.
-Noise is the junk.

Everyone's signal to noise ratio is different. Even a micro difference has a major impact. We are operating with different intentions and desires.

This is also why it's good to always be wary of advice that you're hearing. You don't know if the signal from someone else's life matches the signal for yours.

'What is this *meaningful information*?'
It depends on what you want.

I heard that film directors watch a lot of movies. That is what a large part of their day consists of. That's because film directors make movies. For them, watching movies is a high **ROI** act that fuels creative ideas & angles. That's a signal.

Does that mean watching movies is good advice for someone who has been sitting on their ass binge-watching Netflix movies nonstop? Not quite.

The person watching the nonstop Netflix movies may be watching the same exact movies as the filmmakers, but they are not getting the same results. Why?

Because their intentions are different.

I heard LeBron watches 4 or 5 basketball games at once! That's insane. He said for him, it's like reading a book. It works out his mind.

Tell other people to watch 4 to 5 games at once & they would say:
'What for? I can barely watch 1!'

The main point is that our intentions are different.

'What if I don't have an intention?'
Then 4 possible situations:
-You do not have a signal.
-Your signal is low.
-You mistake noise as signal.
-Your noise is loud.

There are 2 variables in life.
Awareness & nature.

Awareness always is. It is a constant. Nature changes.

Our body, mind & external environment are components of nature. Coming in waves. Up & down. Our awareness just witnesses all of that.

The waves are seen as fun when you have created an intention for yourself. But the waves feel like a pain in the ass, then there was no intention assigned.

That's why the human is always looking for meaning. When we are born into this world, there is no way of running away from nature.

We all have a mind, body & external situations that must be dealt with.

At times, nature is screaming:
'Yo dawg, make sense out of me already! Quit living so day by day! These retirement commercials are lying to you! No sane person just wants to sit on their ass all day drinking on a beach! It's a lie to take away your purpose so these marketing companies can sell you a consumerism lifestyle! Make sense of me already!'

If you didn't read the paragraph above, a summary is...
Nature is guiding your mind to set an intention.
However, we often miss the clues.

Just a general aim.
Work on that aim.

When you set the aim, you can spot the signal from the noise. You stop asking for random book suggestions to feel smart. Instead, you find books that suit your signal.

You stop hanging with losers & reinviting toxic people into your life. Instead, the circle reduces in size & increases in quality.

We have no choice in the game of nature. But we have a choice in the game of setting an intention for our mind. Some grand goal to work towards.

With a strong signal, man & woman can tame nature.

The signal to noise ratio is not only a philosophy for engineers & machines.
It's also a highly practical philosophy for life.

SOCIAL MEDIA'S ROLE ON FRIENDSHIPS

Instagram nowadays has a feature where you can share stories strictly with close friends. Those who marked you as a close friend have a green ring around their profile picture, while all others have a maroon-colored ring.

I was going through my Instagram recently, and I noticed this one kid who I hadn't talked to in years, showed up as a green ring.
He marked me as a close friend.

I felt a good feeling.
The physical sensation.

It reminded me of the Myspace Top 5 or 8 list.
Whatever it was.

What I found odd about this situation was how I was not close with this fellow.
Still, the simple act of classifying me as a close friend was able to create a positive emotion.

The future of friendships and social media is bigger than we think. The role of information systems is going to become a powerful topic.

What separates information systems from traditional technological studies?

Traditional technological studies map humans & technology in their own unique boxes. Information systems combine the 2 groups.

The 3 factors of any information system include:
-Information technology.
-Procedures.
-Humans.

Procedures are mainly prevalent when the piece of technology is complex. It's rarely something that's needed for something like social media. However, you'll often see a guide that shows how everything works when you are first onboarded onto social media.

There was a year in my career when I was a process engineer for an IT company. That's a fancy way of saying that I made procedures so people could operate on the machines.

Nowadays, a company who refuses to onboard the latest technology into their firms are pretty much committing financial suicide. They may soon become irrelevant.

Likewise, not having any social media can lead to a large dark spot in the social life.

I did meet a person not too long ago who was super old fashioned. Pretty young. In his early 30s.

He didn't have Snapchat, Instagram, Facebook, Twitter or any social media for that matter. Just a phone number & email.

It's extremely rare to find people like that nowadays. I'm not saying it's a good thing or a bad thing.

These social media companies are not functioning like a technology company. They are functioning like a psychology company.

How can they keep their users hooked?
What made them install that 'close friends' section?

Scratch that...

Social media companies are not only functioning like a psychology company. They are functioning like a sociology company.

It was the best of times.
It was the worst of times.

The machine-human communication is going to make for an innovative journey into the world of information systems.

We keep hearing:
  o *You are the average of your 5 best friends.*
Soon, we are going to be hearing:
  o *You are the average of the content in your phone.*

Because when you think about it...
Friends are people who you hang out with & eventually say bye to. Your phone stays.

An immature belief is thinking that communication only comes down to words.
That's what low level communicators focus on.

High level communicators focus on the person they are
speaking to.
They factor in the roles of thoughts & emotions of someone
else to best exchange ideas.

*But the top tier communicators are the ones who are capable of
seeing relationships in anything.*

- o Human - animal, aka pet owners & pet.
    - o Why does a pet owner like their pet? It
      doesn't make logical sense. Does it make
      emotional sense?
- o Human - human.
- o The relationship of the items of your living room
  set.
- o Human relationships with their phone.

This seems like a complex way of viewing the world. On
the contrary, to evolve to this stage, you need to go
through the complexity to see the simplicity.

People who view the world through this high-level lens see
utter simplicity and dare I say, beauty.

They see a world of links & nodes.
Links & nodes.
Links & nodes.

Through that utter simplicity, complexity is born. To the
untrained eye, it's scary and messy. To the trained eye,
everything becomes communication.

I LINE HAYMAKER

For me, it's unique when I hear advice that works for someone that also works for me. It's even more unique when I have never met the person. Never knew they existed prior to hearing the advice.

I think:
'How did **2** different people reach the same exact conclusion??'

This has happened a few times and it was spooky. One of the times was with **R.L** Stine. The author of Goosebumps.

My childhood consisted of reading the Goosebumps series. Read that series like I collected Pokémon cards.

I didn't appreciate **R.L** Stine's prolific writing schedule as a kid. I only had the lens of a consumer back then. Not a creator.

I didn't even know what he looked like!

The Goosebumps series had a **TV** show later in the game. However, what really caused this series to spread was the word of mouth. **R.L** rarely did much promotion and media interviews.

As I got older, I recalled **R.L** Stine for some strange reason.
This time, I was able to approach him as a creator, not only a consumer.

How exactly did he write all those books? I believe it's
over a staggering 300! Which is tremendous volume. His
response was very shocking. To me at least.

-He gets the title first.
-Then, he writes the story.

So groundbreaking & unique because it's a strategy that is
not normally leveraged. Just get the title, now you can
reverse engineer it.

Many authors do the opposite. They may get their ending
before their beginning and all of that. But normally, the
title is something they slap on later.

For **R.L Stine**, it was the title first. All else was second.
This was what allowed him to be prolific.

I found this fascinating because that's identical to what I do
with blogs, podcasts and YouTube videos.

Different field.
Identical concept.

How did 2 people reach the same exact path? Doesn't
really matter. This happens in many different fields.

Roy Jones Jr studies animals to improve his boxing style.
He is baffled that other boxers don't do the same. These
fields cross combine.

The question to ask is:
  o   Why the title before the actual work?

I don't know about **R.L** Stine, but I can tell you a reason why I do this strategy.

When I get an idea, it comes in a flash. The whole story is created. By story, I am not talking in terms of content. I am talking in terms of context.

Basically, what is the general gist?

It's a flash that engages my mind and plenty of my senses. That's when I'm like:
- o 'This is what I will talk about today.'

The title trick works because it gets the mind to go straight into the context. What is the general gist, buddy boy? It's easy to focus so much on the content that thinking becomes over thinking.

Plus, with just getting the title, the creator becomes more ninja like. Creativity can be amplified.

It's like a speedboat vs a ship. The speedboat can make a lot of twists and turns. More flexibility.

R.L Stine mentioned how he was one day walking with his son, and someone asked for a picture.

They said, 'say cheese'.
Something like that.

R.L Stine heard, 'say cheese and die.'
Click!
Just got a new book idea.

This title trick may fall flat with a lot of people. I noticed this is a tactic that works with a select group of individuals.

Plus, it's not just limited to writers, podcasters, bloggers etc. Even musicians leverage this trick.

The rapper Future is someone who never plans out anything. He keeps the mind narrow. The narrowed mind becomes expansive.

Concentration and creativity are joined at the hip.

1 line can create a haymaker?
Potentially.

That 1 line is **PURE** potential energy.
What you do with that energy is all up to you.

PUTTING IN YOUR REPS

Picture a scrawny, awkward kid with poor body language. He is around 18 years old & is having a lot of self-doubts recently. No one wants to be his friend, girls don't like him & he gets bullied.

One day, the skinny kid looks in the mirror & realizes exactly what is wrong. He realizes that he looks like a stick.

At that point, he gets an idea. If he can get in shape, then that will end all his troubles!

So, he signs up for his local L.A Fitness & is ready to work out. He is excited to turn his body around so that he can finally become popular.

Once he signs up, he wastes no time putting in work.

He goes over to the bench rack, puts 2, 45-pound plates on each side & gets ready to roll! He makes sure that everyone is watching him as he is about to bench 225-pounds, so they can see what a boss he is.

But as he musters the strength to pick up the weight, the inevitable happens. The barbell slams on his chest & he is unable to move it.

He struggles to get the weight off him, twisting & turning, trying to push it up.

But nothing.

Soon enough, a bodybuilder comes over, picks the weight up with one hand & puts it back on the bench rack.

Everyone is staring at the skinny kid laughing at what they just saw.

The skinny kid is humiliated.

That day, he decides that working out is not for him. He decides that he is going to quit.

Now replace the benching with something that you are currently working on. Is it starting a business, writing a book, building a brand?

If so:
Are you trying to bench 225-pounds too soon?

I knew I used to be like that. I would expect results as soon as I began something. When I didn't see the results in the time frame that my ego had assigned to me, I decided to quit.

Building something that lasts doesn't work like that.
You need to put in your reps.

It's a game of getting the end goal, breaking it into quantifiable segments, & tackling it one at a time.

Instead of seeing a large wall, just see the bricks. Instead of seeing the 225-pounds, see 1 week of repping the bar, 1 week of repping 60-pounds, 1 week of repping 70-pounds and so on...

This sort of mentality shift is what creates a long-term
thinker. Long term thinking makes it easier to deal with
setbacks & recalibrate much smoother.

Whether it's public speaking, storytelling, enhancing
creativity etc.

The reps need to be put in.
Luckily, the reps lead to momentum.
And the momentum is what leads to significant changes.

POWER UP YOUR SOCIAL CIRCLE

I got a call from Harry. He called with pure excitement in his voice.

'Armani, guess what!!'
What?
'I got the job! I'm moving to Virginia next week.'
Whoa, congrats bro! Guess the application finally went through, huh?
'Nope. Doubt they even reviewed my application.'
Wait, what? Then how did you get the job?
'Let's just say I knew someone who knew someone.'

Harry is one of my acquaintances who was frantically searching for a job after graduation. Fortunately, he got his precious job.

However, it wasn't the traditional way through a resume, cover letter, and praying for a phone interview. Instead, it was from a different method.

It was through his network.
What is a network?

In the technical world, a network is an interconnection of nodes that can communicate with one another.

Picture the internet.
My computer is a node.
Your computer is a node.

Through the link, I can email you.

Same concept in the real world.

Jimmy is a node.
Tommy is a node.
When Jimmy says hello to Tommy, he sparks a possible link.

Want to know something even cooler?

When Jimmy says hello to Tommy, he has the potential to be connected with many of the nodes that Tommy knows as well! That is the power of a network.

In my friend Harry's case, he didn't particularly know anyone in the company that hired him. But his cousin Rohit sure did.

Once Rohit found out that Harry needed a job, he made a few calls to his buddy Mike. Mike loves Rohit & knew that his referral meant something. And just like that, Mike short-circuited Harry through the resume & cover letter process & got him an interview.

'How does someone power up their social circle?'
Have more acquaintances.

'Are friends & acquaintances the same?'
Nope.

You have a deeper connection with a friend. Mostly informal. You have an intermediate level connection with an acquaintance. In many cases, formal.

'Why not just have a bunch of friends?'
Because you can have deep connections with just so many
people. But after a while, you get burnt out & fail to be a
top-notch friend.

Instead, have a small friend circle, nurture deep bonds, and
then have a large acquaintance circle & nurture the bonds
so it remains relevant.

Acquaintances can be more powerful for long-term goals
than friends. Chances are you know a lot of your friends,
friends. But for acquaintances, they have a whole new
network than you. And with acquaintances, they don't
really care if you are calling them every day. Just a text
once or a few times a month should do the trick.

So, what does this all mean?
It means that a simple 'hello' can connect your node to a
brand-new network.

In the world of networks & systems, nonlinear effects take
place. The world of nonlinearity is much different from
linearity.

It's easy to rule of the 'hello' as being a small move.
However, that small move can compound into something
big. Harry didn't get his job by playing the formal rules.
He got his job by going beyond the rules.

An acquaintance is nothing to scoff at. The acquaintance is
born from a win-win relationship. A win-win relationship
which will pay dividends for years to come.

CONSISTENCY

Whenever I visit my parents in West Palm Beach, I go watch a movie with my mom. My dad doesn't like movies too much. So it's a mother-son bonding moment.

One of the movies we watched was a Sylvester Stallone movie.
Rambo the Last blood.

'How was it?'
It was very good.

What was baffling about it was that in the end of the movie, they did a little highlight reel of Sylvester's past Rambo movies. He has been at it with writing & acting for decades. Producing hit after hit.

This got me thinking.
If Sylvester Stallone can be so consistent, why not others?

It's because Sylvester Stallone is a creator. He has fun doing what he has been doing. That's why what most people in the Hollywood industry consider difficult, he considers 2nd nature.

I'm no movie producer or script writer, so I find his task to feel like work. While in his world, he has fun doing it & it feels hard for him to quit. That's why years later, in his 60s, he still is not stopping.

The movie was titled, The Last Blood. But I don't think it will be the last of Stallone. I think he is going to be coming in with another hit, whether it's Rambo or something else.

What can Stallone teach us about creativity?

He is teaching us to zone in on the task which makes us feel like Stallone when he's making Rocky & Rambo.

The goal is to zone in. Zoning in requires simplicity. Yet, there is a problem. In school, we were given a bunch of subjects to learn. So, a part of us may feel guilty when we are simplifying everything down to 1-2 things. It's as though we are not working hard enough. But no.

That's you directing your energy vs spreading it thin. Simplify.

Simplification is what allows someone to be consistent for so many years. When you simplify, you become more creative at the task. Which allows you to produce more with less.

It's a chain effect of productivity.

If you have been finding it difficult to be consistent, then take a few steps back. Now cut out the crap & obsess over the rest.

- o Steve Jobs dropped all the products except 3 when making his return to Apple.
- o Dirk Nowitzki had a singular focus on basketball for 20 years.

o   Alexander the Great wanted to be the greatest ruler of all time.

Less is more.
That's the rule of consistency.

THE HIDDEN POWER OF WALKING

In my last job, my company had this huge pathway in the
back of our building. 2 laps equaled a mile.

I used to listen to music and walk there.
I had this entire pathway to myself.
It felt like a personal kingdom.

Until things changed.
'What changed?'
Others had discovered the pathway.

You'll be surprised by how many people walk slow as shit.
Dragging their feet.
Moping around.
o urgency.

So rather than just walking now, *I was walking and
weaving.*

The walking did not end with work. It was a habit picked
up at work and continued at home. Every morning, go for a
walk & get the day started Armani.

'Why did you decide to walk with intent?'
I have o clue.

Just got a hunch one day & began.
I didn't think much of this hunch.

As some time passed by, I saw documentaries which
mentioned that a lot of intellectual giants had a walking
habit.

Apparently, Isaac Newton used to do it.
Nikola Tesla.
Mark Twain was in the walking club.

That's when I became intrigued. Why did so many people
walk with intent?

I think I have a clue, but no way to prove it.

A lot of our primal ancestors leveraged walking to get from
point A to point B. They weren't driving, of course. I
doubt they were running all the time. They would
mainly run when they had to hunt or were escaping from a
predator.

During the Ice Age, a lot of the world had united.

The frozen water served as a bridge to get from one point
to another. Once again, walking was leverage.

In my eyes, walking is a tool to program the mind to enter
the unknown.

Whenever you leverage mystery, you get creativity. There
has not been one creative person who didn't have a sense of
wonder.

That's why *know it all's* are annoying to be around. They
think they are sooo smart. But they aren't saying anything
unique.

Walking consistently gets the mind to favor consistency over everything else. Not everyone does sprints on a consistent basis. At times, our joints hurt.

But with walking?
Anyone can put one foot in front of the other.

How you put that foot in front of the other displays the intent that you operate life with.
- o   Dragging feet?
- o   Or purposeful strides?

Walking is for the body as what journaling is for the mind. It helps a person serve as an antenna for the universe.

When you visualize, walk.
When you have writer's block, walk.
When you feel lazy, walk.

It's the best kept secret out there. Although, it's never been a secret.

AFTERWARD

Do you recall the first time you ever learned how to drive? There was a moment when I witnessed someone learning to drive for the first time.

This was when my friend ended up taking his parents car for a late-night drive. Let's call this friend, Rahul.

Rahul had his younger brother in the car and picked me up as well. So, there were 3 people in this Toyota Camry. Seeing Rahul drive was a cool experience. We were both 17 at the time and had just gotten our licenses. The whole act of driving was a rather new experience.

Rahul's little brother, Sam, wanted to drive, but he was only 15. He kept asking Rahul to see if he could get behind the wheel. Each time, Rahul firmly said no.

Eventually, Rahul drove to his girlfriend's apartment and said that he was going to chill with her for 20 minutes. He gave me the keys and said to cruise around. But whatever I do, don't let his little brother drive the car.

Just 20 minutes, what's the worst that could happen?

After Rahul left, Sam gave a plea for why he should drive the car. He had been waiting for this moment for a long time. He was 15 and so close to getting his license.

'Just 2 minutes,' he asked.

I heard Sam's plea and I could feel the exact same emotions he was feeling. 2 years before, I was making the same request to my older brother.

The younger brother in me resonated with the younger brother in Sam. At that point, I said, 'Okay, just drive in a straight line so you get a feeling for what driving is like.' This was late at night, and no one would know. It was quiet and everyone was sleeping.

Sam's eyes lit up.

I get in the back seat for some reason instead of the passenger seat and Sam comes up to the driver's seat.

He puts the key in turns it, goes on 'drive' and.... JAMS HIS FOOT ON THE ACCELERATOR.

Just like that, the car abruptly drives forward and is put into motion. I began screaming, 'Sam, don't hit the accelerator so hard. Slow down, slow down, slow down!!!'

I guess my gut must have known what was going to happen, which is why I went to the backseat instead of the passenger seat. However, Sam's foot was still heavy on the accelerator.

'Slow down Sam, slow down!!!' I screamed.
Suddenly, CRASH!
Sam had crashed into a fence.

That's when from the corner of my eye, I see a man waving a flashlight looking to see what was going on.

I was angry at Sam. I put my hand on his shoulder from the backseat and asked, 'What the hell, why did you do that? Why did you go so fast, dumbass?'

Luckily for the both of us, the flashlight man disappeared. But my anger with Sam was at an all-time high.

Afterwards, Rahul comes downstairs and is furious at me for allowing his younger brother to drive. He kept saying, 'told you so.'

Rahul deserved to be mad. I was an idiot.

That moment taught me the importance of not allowing someone to go for a joy ride. It also taught me that things look easier from the outside than the inside.

After Sam had gotten behind the wheel, he saw firsthand the level of balance, precision, and cognition it takes for a newbie driver to learn the vehicle. After that moment, I'm sure Sam learned that driving wasn't all that easy.

Is there a field that you think looks easy?
Did you ever consider that it seems so simple because you are a Sam in the situation?

I had this moment myself with YouTube. Thought it was easy to set up a channel. You just turn the camera on and talk. What could be so difficult about that?

Well, I was proven wrong.

Doing a YouTube video requires a balance of mind and body. Some people can talk into a camera for a large period of time.

This shows concentration, articulation skills and creativity. That's the soft side of it. In terms of the physiological aspects? The body can tense up, breathing can become shallow, and the mouth can become dry.

It's almost impossible to know how difficult it is to do a 10-minute talk, uninterrupted (no editing out the mistakes), without doing it for yourself.

That's why the concept of street smarts has always resonated with me.

I was an average student from kindergarten to high school. By undergrad, I became better. However, I was not great. By the time I went from undergrad to grad school, my grades had skyrocketed. I wondered why?

The reason why was because in my bachelor's, I had a lot of exams. Always hated exams and the nerves it would generate in me. In master's, there were more team projects and less exams. This simple shift in curriculum explained why my grades had evolved.

The process of working in a team is a process of looking into the real world.

Some teammates work hard, while some are lazy. Some can make it on a Sunday, Tuesday and Friday for the meetings, while other members are the busiest on those days. Now it's a process of finding a middle ground that works for all the members. There are times team members argue on the smallest things.

All these variables make the street smarts aspect of group projects very volatile. With volatility, comes a high potential for success.

In this book, hopefully you learned concepts of street smarts that you haven't heard of too much before. This field and most of informal education is not something that has been formalized. It's something where people learn along the way and share their insights along the way.

As I get older, a part of me is proud of Sam for asking to drive the car. That's not right of me to say. However, I liked his guts. The kid was brave for a 15-year-old.

Bravery is hard to measure in quantifiable stages. It's because no one can feel our emotions for us. It's something that we experience ourselves.

What is light work for one person is hard work for another and *vice versa*.

Street smarts and introspection go hand in hand. Learn how you work so you find the fears worth tackling.

If you enjoyed my writing style and the short stories, be sure to follow me further on www.armanitalks.com.

In this website, you'll get a centralized look of all of my content ranging from YouTube videos, podcasts, blogs, Twitter and other books. In addition, you can join the www.armanitalks.com/newsletter where I deliver you a brand-new short story every day.

A tiny tale is a lost art. However, I see it making a comeback in this globalized era that we are living in. The world is getting busy and for many, attentions spans are getting lower. A short story not only teaches, but it teaches effectively.

The ArmaniTalks brand is built from short stories designed to help you build your communication skills. The package of communicating with confidence is what allows the isolated concepts of street smarts to become one grand web.

In this web, you will rewire neural pathways in new ways. Within this web, you will meet people you never thought you would meet and read the works of authors who you never thought you would read.

Book smarts is never vilified in this side of the world. It serves as the magnifier when the foundations have been laid.

However, let's not forget, there is a leader. Street smarts is the philosophy that leads the subtle decisions which seem so difficult from the outside.

Do now, ask questions later.
Take tactical risks rather than foolish ones.
All experiences have silver linings, and no experience will ever be bad if you found that silver lining.

Learn in the streets and have an intellect that cannot be questioned. That's the brain and heart working with one another, rather than fighting.
Best wishes.

ARMANITALKS